W9-BZU-120

THE SPIRITUAL JOURNEY OF
J.C. PENNEY

THE SPIRITUAL JOURNEY OF
J.C. PENNEY

Orlando L. Tibbetts

Rutledge Books, Inc.

Danbury, CT

Copyright © 1999 by Orlando L. Tibbetts

ALL RIGHTS RESERVED
Rutledge Books, Inc.
107 Mill Plain Road, Danbury, CT 06811
1-800-278-8533
www.rutledgebooks.com

Manufactured in the United States of America

Cataloging in Publication Data
Tibbetts, Orlando L.
   The Spiritual Journey of J.C. Penney

   ISBN: 1-58244-038-7

   1. Penney, J.C. (James Cash), 1875-1971.
2. Spirituality.   3. Business.
658.27

To

Phyllis Jones Tibbetts,

my wife,

who has loved and supported me

under all circumstances.

CONTENTS

ACKNOWLEDGMENTS

A BOOK IS NEVER WRITTEN BY ONE PERSON. MANY PEOPLE BECOME involved and help to provide the facts and information which eventually put words on the pages. This has happened during the many months I spent in telling the fascinating story of J.C. Penney.

I am most grateful to the following, with the hope that I have not left someone out who played a part in creating this book:

Dr. W. Hubert Porter has been an invaluable partner in sharing the archives which he has collected throughout his years at the Penney Retirement Community (PRC); likewise Dr. Kenneth Wilson, former editor of the *Christian Herald* and member of the PRC Board of Directors, has provided wisdom and guidance; Dr. Paul Hagen, former chief administrator of PRC provided help from his memories of the early days of Mr. Penney's life; Sarah Elsesser, librarian of the PRC Library; and the staff of the Green Cove Springs Library all provided me with resources. Likewise, Daisy Keller, Archivist of PRC, made records and papers available to me.

Some of the early residents during the time when Mr. Penney established his presence in northeast Florida who were among the many persons I interviewed and received material to make this book were: Mr. Job Travassos, who lived with his family on one of the first farms at Long Branch (which was later named Penney Farms); the Reverend James Saunders whose roots go back to the early Penney Farm days where he lived and attended school, ran a general store and later became mayor of the town; his wife, Mitzi, who presently serves as Postmistress of the town, shared additional memories concerning life after Mr. Penney established the farms and the retirement community; Hilda Summersill, a present resident of PRC, grew up in Green Cove Springs and provided historical background for this story; Mr. William Kinney, who served for a number of years as the Finance Controller of PRC and his wife, Betty, former president of the Clay County Historical Society, each gave color to some of what I have written; Tom DeVille, a resident of Penney Farms, former mayor of the town and present member of the Town Council, took me to the ruins of the early town farm houses and shared information and knowledge of the past history; Betty Thomas, secretary of the Shadowlawn office in Penney Farms, helped me to discover things about the Penney Farm experiment; Dr. Howard Tappan, Music Director at the Penney Memorial Church, provided historical material; Marion Meyer, present president of the church board, supplied audio tapes recorded by church members who have passed on; Ellen Gustafson Townsend of Green Cove Springs whose family established the Gustafson's Dairy Farm before Mr. Penney came to Green Cove Springs; Florence McClelland loaned me tapes by former residents, including a tape made by Mr. Penney in 1934; Margaret Lake, resident of the community, whose husband was an executive of the American Bible Society, supplied me with information about Mr. Penney's relationship with the American Bible Society; Margaret Smith, energetic member of the PRC Board of Directors, steered me toward people who could be interviewed; Lester Smith, long time resident of PRC, who once worked in a Penney store and knew its owner; Dr. Noel White, Administrator and President of PRC, encouraged me to write this book and contributed the photo of Mr. Penney for use on the book's cover.

I want to especially thank my wife, Phyllis, for her love and patience during the long months that it took to write this book. I also want to thank J. Carol Freehan, who typed all my previous books and who worked hard to translate my handwritten manuscript for her computer. Finally I want to express my appreciation to Arthur Salzfass, president of Rutledge Books, Inc., who enthusiastically saw the potential in this book and helped me to see it published.

FOREWORD

THIS BOOK CAME INTO BEING BECAUSE OF THE APPROACHING 75TH anniversary of the establishment of Penney Retirement Community by Mr. J.C. Penney in 1926.

After months of diligent research through books and files, it began to dawn upon me that Mr. Penney's spiritual life had never been adequately revealed. I was convinced that the spiritual history and philosophy of this great man was a story to be told.

In a time when spirituality is of such great interest to so many people, I found myself drawn into a deeper revelation of this person who was more than an industrial great.

James Cash Penney was a seeker of the reality of God for himself, his family and his business. As he struggled through physical and psychological problems, through historical happenings like the Great Depression, two world wars, and the losing of two of his wives through tragic deaths, he was always threatened by the quicksand of insecurity, but he never gave up his search for the Rock upon which his parents had stood through their trying years.

It also occurred to me during this research time that the contributions and significances of his three wives, who influenced him during his ascension to greatness in America's twentieth century, had not been fully shared.

Because this is being written as a fictional biography, much of what I have written concerning his early days, his business associates, and those who were a part of his early endeavors in Florida are a product of my creative imagination which was based upon true historical fact. I have tried to be faithful to the actual spirit of the man and the contributions he made.

The bottom line concerning the spiritual journey of J.C. Penney was his ability to manifest the relationship between his faith and his actions.

During a celebration of his ninety-fifth birthday at the American Bible Society, someone is quoted as saying, "More than his words, his life was his message."

May the words I have written be transformed into a portrait of a mighty life which will inspire.

INTRODUCTION

A NUMBER OF THE CHAPTERS OF THIS BOOK WERE WRITTEN DURING my vacation stay at beautiful Lake Junaluska snuggled in the foothills of the Smoky Mountains of North Carolina. I sit at a desk writing where, as I glance up, I'm inspired by the panorama I see through the large windows overlooking the lake. On this spectacular location, the United Methodists established a significant assembly grounds modeled after the Chatauqua Center in New York State. The founding of this assembly happened around the same time that a young man named James Cash Penney was establishing a new chain of stores which would be located in every area of the United States.

At Lake Junaluska there are all the usual places found in a Chatauqua-like setting: the large circular auditorium which seats two thousand, the inns built in charming southern style, the modern Terrace Hotel with dining room, meeting rooms for conferences, the Memorial Chapel still serving its purpose from early days, and a number of other centers, each with facilities for enabling visitors to experience inspiration and growth.

Among the buildings overlooking the lake and the inspiring mountains is a place called "The Intentional Growth

Center." The name of the place, which carries on a program of continuing education on a national scale, including elder hostels, leads me to link the idea of intentional growth to the man I am writing about. For one of the central aspects of the life of James Cash Penney was his constant desire for intentional growth. He applied this to his own life, to the stores he established in communities everywhere, and to the founding of the Penney Retirement Community seventy-five years ago.

The idea of creating a community for retired senior adults came to Mr. Penney in a God-given way. Though he may not have been aware of its future significance for older people, he was setting in motion a place modeled after his own life.

Based upon the Golden Rule, the retirement village which bears his name was put on the road to becoming a place for intentional growth. Just as his life was a model of intentional growth until the day he died, the Penney Retirement Community became, while being one of the best kept secrets in the country, a model for intentional growth. It possessed the clue to meaningful, happy, golden years.

The story I am sharing about this great man is more than a tribute to an outstanding business mogul. It is a sharing of an inspirational life driven by a dream which was never diminished by advancing years. Hopefully it is a story which will enable many to seek out ways of growing with confidence, while discovering the joy which comes from serving others.

Chapter I

The Discovery of Gold

Rain pounded on the roof of the barn where the eight-year-old Jim Penney sat on a stool next to his father in the milking room. The boy was milking his favorite cow named Blossom. The warmth of the animal's body sent off steam which enveloped the boy as his father glanced over from his stall, while rhythmically milking Blossom's sister, who had recently delivered a new calf to the Penney family.

"Son," inquired the boy's father, "do I see you sitting there doing your chores in your stocking feet?"

"Yes, sir," answered the boy, glancing fearfully at his father who was the strict disciplinarian who wouldn't be pleased with a son taking off his shoes while in a dark, damp barn. "I had to because my shoes have holes in the soles and I had put some cardboard in to come over from the house. But the cardboard got soaked and I had to take the shoes off."

"Once we get these cows milked I want you to come into

my study. I've got some very important things to talk over with you."

"Yes, sir, I'll be there," said Jim, wondering what would be the purpose of seeing his father in the study. It usually meant he'd done something wrong and would get a lecture. But, what had he done to displease his father? Was it the shoes? Often, after the first of May he went around the farm barefooted. He'd only worn those shoes because of the heavy rains.

Later, after cleaning up and putting dry pieces of newspaper in his shoes, Jim Penney knocked on the closed door of the study of the Rev. James Penney who rarely let the children into this sacred place where he prepared his soul for the daily ministry at Hamilton, Missouri.

"Come in, son," invited the father, and watched the boy slip into the caned chair in front of his desk.

"I'm sure you're wondering why I've asked you to come see me here. It's not because of anything you've done but because you're growing up. Now that you're eight years old I think it's time to tell you that your mother and I are having a difficult time feeding and dressing all you children. I've decided that you should now be buying your own clothes...and I saw the problem you're having with those shoes...and, Jimmy, I can't help you."

"You mean that you can't buy me a new pair of shoes?" the boy asked in an agonizing voice.

"That's right. You've got to find a way to earn more money and buy them yourself."

The boy couldn't believe what he was hearing. Neither

did he have any idea how he could earn more money to purchase his own clothes.

The next day the enterprising young Penney came up with an idea. Since the melons in their crop had been the best in many seasons, he would use the family wagon and take some to the upcoming County Fair and sell them to the crowds that came from all over the county.

On the following Saturday, Jim Penney was one of the first to arrive at the County Fair gate. As he saw the price of entrance posted for those who would exhibit or sell, he realized he did not have the cash available to take his wagon loaded with the delicious melons inside. So, he parked the horse and wagon down the road and called out to people as they approached the gate.

The response was good. Many people stopped their buggies and bought a lot of the melons. Then, one carriage pulled up by him and a man jumped down and grabbed the boy by the shoulders. "What are you doing?" he shouted, as he shook the frightened boy.

"I'm earning money to buy me some new shoes," answered the boy in a quivering voice.

"But you don't earn money doing something illegal," said his father between clenched teeth.

"I'm not doing anything illegal, father," answered the boy respectfully.

"Perhaps you're not breaking a law of the country but you are breaking a law of good will. The people selling inside that gate have paid a fee to sell. You have paid nothing out here as you take advantage of them. Would you want them to do that to you, if you were inside? Remember, as long as you live, God's Word tells us to do to others what we'd want them to do to us."

This experience never left him, as J.C. Penney entered his boyhood years which were filled with a mixture of discoveries and discouragements. The discoveries were made when his father lectured him on life. Once he sat with the boy and tried to motivate him with a lecture on the value of hard work.

Sitting in his study with the boy at his knees the wise father said, "Jim, we are so fortunate that God has given us these acres of land to farm. But if you hope to get somewhere in your future, you will have to work hard. You will have to dig. You will have to plant. You will have to cultivate and you will have to stay up nights."

The boy listened intently, wondering, at the same time, whether he would decide to be a farmer for the rest of his life.

His father continued, "You must learn to do things for yourself. And, son, what I'm telling you is worth a college education. I'm offering you advice, free, and experience you can't get anywhere else."

Young Jim appreciated what his father was sharing and, especially, though Dad wanted him to be a farmer, his insistence that he go to high school and get as much education as they could afford.

On another day, with another lecture from Dad, young Jim heard him say, "Always remember, Jim, that God will allow for your mistakes and will balance them out of the goodness of His inexhaustible supply. All that He requires of

4

you is that you meet His minimum terms. And those minimum terms are in a contract called the 'Golden Rule.' These words were etched into the depth of the boy's mind. He never forgot them.

The years ahead were also filled with discouragement. The greatest of negative experiences for the family was a meeting of the church where a relative of Pastor James C. Penney made a motion that their minister be expelled from the ministry because of his heretical ideas about the ministry. To the disappointment of the Penney family, the vote was carried to its completion and the Rev. Mr. Penney was forced to give up his leadership and give full attention to his farming. Though the church did not believe in paying their pastor, they had compensated him with food and sometimes with clothing. This ended and cast a heavy burden upon the ex-pastor and his large family.

Having left the ministry, the elder Penney decided to enter the field of politics. In the years 1890-1894 he ran for Congress on three different ballots and lost them all. Through all this the younger Penney saw his father stand strong and tenacious. This example of his father being persecuted by the so-called religious and still holding to his convictions without bitterness or retribution impressed the son. He saw his father maintaining with steadfastness the Golden Rule principle. This shaped the thinking of young James Cash Penney for the rest of his days.

Not too long after the dismissal by the church and the losses at the polls, James Cash Penney, Sr., began to fail in health. While on his deathbed, he called his children to his side. One by one, he held their hands and gave them final counsel.

Young Jim sat at his father's side and with tears streaming down his checks listened to his father who, in a weakened voice, told him that he had talked with J.M. Hale, of the store J.M. Hale and Brother. He pleaded with Mr. Hale to teach young Jim the business of merchandising, and, though Mr. Hale didn't need another clerk, he was willing to make his contribution to his friend's life.

The dying father urged Jim to be open to Mr. Hale's offer, even though it meant getting very little financial remuneration. To be associated with such a dry goods store as J.M. Hale's, in Hamilton, Missouri, would be better than a college education. He didn't admit to his son what he felt as he talked with Mr. Hale. He knew the store president had heard that the elder Penney was in ill health. He realized that he was offering Jim a job because he felt sorry for his father.

Some weeks later the elder Penney breathed his last and the widow Mary Frances Penney, stood at the open grave with her seven children. She was remembering the other five who had been buried before growing up. She sobbed with the ache of heart and loneliness of spirit as young Jim put his arm around his frail mother's waist. He was trying to assure her that he would become her loving support. They rode back from the snow-covered cemetery in the family wagon feeling the emptiness of their lives as the awareness of their loss pressed in upon them. The coldness of the winter wind engulfed young Jim as he felt the first waves of anxiety about showing up at the J.M. Hale and Brother's store that next week in February of 1895.

It was a dark, ominous day when Jim trudged up to the store wearing his late father's overcoat, at the insistence of his mother. When he entered a clerk asked if he could help him.

"I'm looking for Mr. Hale who is expecting me," said the young man noticing that the clerk grimaced and pointed toward a desk in the corner of the store. Without saying another word, the clerk turned angrily and went toward the front of the store. Jim was soon to discover that the senior worker would rally the other clerks against the new intruder.

Mr. Hale received the young Penney with almost the same negative attitude that the other workers had manifested. Sitting at his desk without getting up and looking over the glasses on the end of his nose, the owner said coldly, "I told your father before he died that I would take you on because he was a friend, but all I can pay you is $2.27 a month." Then he pointed to the grumpy senior clerk who had directed Jim to him. "He'll show you what to do." And that's how young J.C. Penney began his career as a dry goods clerk.

The next few months for Jim Penney were filled with hurt and pain as the clerks at the store did everything to make his life miserable. But, drawing upon the residual tenacity that he had seen in his father, he refused to be vanquished by these people. They were threatened by the bright young preacher's son.

After almost a year of taking abuse from his insecure fellow workers, and remembering what his father had taught him about the Golden Rule, the young Penney worked more intensely at learning the clothing and dry goods business. He also remembered his father's sermons and the personal example of "going the second mile." He would show them, without bitterness or retaliation, what he could do. And he did! So much so that Mr. Hale warmed up to him and not only gave him a raise in salary but began to teach him some of the secrets of good management that even the other clerks did not know.

In his third year at J.M. Hale and Brother, Jim Penney established himself as a superior clerk and a pleasant personality to work with. But this job pressure began to take its toll. He finally went to see a family doctor, at his mother's insistence. The physical examination showed that the pale, thin young store clerk was having breathing problems. The doctor was concerned that he might be on the verge of a tuberculosis infection. Consumption was prevalent in that area.

"You've got to get out of that closed-up store and get a job out in the fresh air," the doctor advised as he hung his stethoscope around his neck. He looked seriously at Jim while the boy buttoned his shirt. "My advice to you is not only to quit working in that store but you should move out of the moist Missouri air."

Jim looked devastated as he asked, "And where would you have me go, Doctor?"

The doctor scratched his head and said, "All my medical colleagues are urging people in your condition to head for Colorado. If I were you, I wouldn't wait very long to do that!"

That night at the supper table, Jim shared with his mother what the doctor had advised. She could sense, through the tone of his voice, that he was not fully convinced he should make such a radical move.

With a reassuring voice, and reaching to take his hand, she said, "Jim, God may be in this. All things work for good to those who love God. Do what the doctor advises."

"But, Mother," he pleaded, "I can't leave you and the others. My salary is what has kept us going."

"Yes, son, but thanks to you and your father's foresight, we've sold almost 30,000 bushels of corn and at the highest price we've ever received. The mortgage has been reduced with the extra money. We've never been in a better financial position. Besides, I trust God that we will be taken care of."

At that moment young J.C. Penney seemed to feel the hand of his father upon his shoulder affirming what his mother had just said.

"I'll do it!" he exclaimed as he got up from the table to reach for the coffeepot sitting on the kitchen stove. "I'll tell Mr. Hale tomorrow morning that I have no choice, and I'll be on a train headed for Colorado within a day or two!"

"Good for you, my darling," exclaimed his mother as she rose to hug her son. She knew everything was going to be all right.

As the train pulled into Denver with Jim Penney aboard, the young adventurer thought of the earlier gold rush to this part of the world in 1849. Though the wooden passenger car in which he rode the distance from Missouri to this high sierra city was uncomfortably hot, most of the way he realized that he was lucky not to be climbing those heights in a covered wagon. He also felt the freshness and coolness of the mountain air as the train wove its way among the awesome peaks and canyons. What was ahead for him? Had he done the right thing in leaving his job at the J.M. Hale and Brother company? He remembered his father's advice to be willing to work hard, trust God and live the right life. All would be well.

Upon descending from the railroad coach with the hurrying passengers, he asked the conductor to point him toward the commercial section of Denver where he might find a dry goods store. With his heavy suitcase in hand he walked to the place indicated by the kind conductor. One of the first signs he saw was for a dry goods store called Joslin Dry Goods Company. He found the office of the store, explained his desire for a job and how much experience he had had at the store in Missouri. They hired him for $6.00 a week and then he set out to find a room. Some blocks away he inquired at several rooming houses only to find that life was far more expensive in Denver than at home. So, he finally chose a room for $4.50 a week which didn't leave him much for food.

He was happy to have a job and to feel the immediate benefits of the high altitude air.

The next day, after a restless night, he appeared at the dry goods store which had hired him the day before, and presented himself to the manager. This man was a gruff, overweight, foul-mouthed type who turned him over to an assistant. Jim felt the assistant could become a friend, as he felt comfortable with him.

Only a few weeks passed before the new young clerk was experiencing "deja vu." Some of the competitive attitudes manifested in his previous job began to appear. The clerks organized an informal, quiet but hostile relationship with Jim and this caused him to anguish over his next steps. What really became a problem for him was the practice of "double-pricing." Two prices were put on the goods with instructions to sell for the higher price but if the customer wouldn't buy then they would sell at a lesser price. This bothered Jim Penney as he felt it to be unethical. After discussing this with the manager, who laughed at him for his insistence upon honesty, Jim announced that he was quitting and wanted his paycheck for the weeks he'd worked.

During the next days he pounded the dusty streets of Denver looking for a new job. With nothing in sight and his money beginning to disappear he bought a few newspapers from Denver and surrounding towns.

On the advertising page of the main newspaper of Longmont, a small town forty miles north of Denver, he read an intriguing ad. A butcher shop was for sale. The asking price was within reach of his $300.00 savings which he had left behind in the bank of Missouri.

The young Penney wired his mother telling of the new potential for buying the butcher shop and asking her to withdraw his $300.00 savings and mail it to him.

He visited Longmont, negotiated with the owner of the meat shop, and checked out the town, discovering that it had more of the small town flavor that he was accustomed to in his home town. He was convinced that a big city like Denver was not for him. Besides, Longmont seemed friendlier, and the whole environment healthier than Denver.

He was extremely excited when his money arrived, and he took over the butcher shop with the help of the chief butcher who stayed on to share his expertise. One of the first things he did was to get a sign made by a Longmont sign-maker which said, "J.C. Penney." He hung it outside with pride.

The Longmont Hotel was the chief customer of the Penney Butcher Shop but, to Jim Penney's dismay, he found there was a practice of bribing the cook at the hotel in order to get their meat orders. The cook insisted upon being paid in whiskey. The influence of J.C. Penney, Sr., and his stance against drinking or selling liquor, gave young Jim sleepless nights. One morning he awakened determined to stop the "bourbon payoff" to the hotel cook. Once done, the orders for meat for the Longmont Hotel ceased and the butcher shop had to close.

Just a few blocks from the butcher shop was a store called The Golden Rule Store, which Jim Penney had visited several times while struggling over what to do with his butcher shop. The smell of the clothes, the sight of familiar decorations, and the counters covered with familiar clothing brought back all the residual desires to be in a working place where he felt at home.

Penney made an appointment with T.M. Callahan, who was the owner of The Golden Rule Store. As the two men sat at the owner's desk he looked at Jim and said, "Didn't I see you working at the butcher shop?"

"Yes, sir," responded the job-seeker, "I've been there for several months."

"Well, son," said Mr. Callahan, as he rose from his chair, as if to indicate that the interview was over, "two things I need to tell you. First, I don't have an opening for a clerk, and second, I sure don't need a meat-cutter working at The Golden Rule."

"But," persisted Penney, without getting up from his chair, "you might need someone soon and I think you should know that I'm not a butcher. I just spent my life savings to hold myself over and I believe I was led to you."

"Led to me," laughed the store owner, "by whom and by what?" With this he sat down again, intrigued by the persistence of the job-seeker who seemed to be on the edge of desperation.

Jim Penney paused for a few moments, thought a quiet prayer and then answered the query.

"I came to Colorado for two reasons. One, because my doctor ordered me to come and secondly because I want to be a dry goods worker. But, I probably made a mistake in buying that butcher shop. Even though I did that I was drawn to your store by the name, The Golden Rule Store."

"Why would that interest you?" broke in Mr. Callahan, sensing that the young job-seeker was on the verge of sharing something important.

Feeling that Callahan was ready to hear what he had bottled-up within, Jim Penney told him how his father had instilled within him, as a boy, the need for living by the Golden Rule. As he spoke, the owner looked deeply into Jim's eyes and seemed impressed by the young man from Missouri.

"I'll tell you what," said Mr. Callahan, "it's true I don't have an opening right now but I feel you are being honest with me and have been led to me by God."

With this Jim straightened up, breathed deeply, and smiled. At that moment he felt the presence of God with him and the hand of his late father upon him once again.

Mr. Callahan informed Penney that one of his clerks was sick with the flu and, because Christmas was approaching, he needed a temporary replacement.

"If you want to help me out until he recovers and returns, I will put you to work beginning tomorrow."

Young Penney ran almost all the way back to his room with excitement filling his breast and the great desire to write his mother about the good news. Even though this was a temporary job he felt sure that some good would come from it. "Most of all," he wrote his mother that night, "I'm going to be in a store called 'The Golden Rule Store' and it seems that Papa has been looking down upon me and is smiling happily because his son is now given a new opportunity to live out the Golden Rule with a man who reminds me of him."

When the Christmas shopping season was ended, Mr. Callahan called Penney to his office and expressed his pleasure with the new worker's performance. Then he explained that, though he didn't need him in Longmont, one of his partners had charge of a store in Evanston, Colorado. He told Jim that he was just the kind of person he would like to put with his Evanston manager.

While Penney was trying to catch his breath and slow his

pounding heart he blurted out his eagerness to accept the position in Evanston.

Jim heard Callahan share his dream of having a chain of Golden Rule stores, modeled after the Longmont store. It was the first time that young Penney had ever heard of a chain of stores. The concept gripped him and little did T.M. Callahan dream what that idea would do to motivate this young blossoming merchant.

The next day when J.C. Penney returned to get further instructions about traveling to Evanston, contacting Mr. Johnson, the partner in charge of the new store, and even taking some important documents to the man who was to become his new boss and mentor, he thanked Mr. Callahan for the confidence he had in him.

The last thing Mr. Callahan said to Penney as he left him to take the train out of the Denver station was, "Mr. Penney, there's something about you that makes me feel good." Gripping his hand in a warm farewell, he added, "You come up to my expectations and there's a good chance that I can put you in charge of one of the new stores I hope to open up soon. If I do that you can be one of my partners in the Golden Rule chain."

With this good news lifting his spirits, as the train pulled out of Denver on the way to Evanston, Jim Penney looked out the coach windows at the beautiful, purple-blue mountains. He saw the snowcapped peaks, with the golden rays of sun tinting them. He lifted his soul up to God in prayer. His adventuresome journey to Colorado had resulted in his discovery of gold!

CHAPTER II

REACHING FOR THE STARS

BERTA SAT ON THE PORCH OF THE WOODEN-FRAME HOUSE ROCKING vigorously in an old, creaking rocking chair. Her feet could barely stretch to the floor because of her tiny, five-foot-three frame. She gasped for the mountain air as another asthma attack forced her outside in anticipation of her husband's coming home from the store. Darkness was settling over the Main Street cottage in Evanston which she and Jim had rented some months before.

Suddenly she detected his form approaching through the purple shadows. She stood up to greet him with outstretched arms. He stopped on the middle step and contemplated the woman before him.

She was a pretty woman, dressed in one of his store's pink gingham dresses. His heart went out to her as it had when he first saw her in Longmont that eventful day when she came into The Golden Rule Store to make a purchase. At that time she appeared to him like a tragic princess who had just learned of the death of her prince in battle.

One of the clerks knew Berta Alva Hess and had advised Jim Penney to forget her because she was a "divorced" woman. Her marriage at age nineteen had ended as a childless mistake. But Jim saw something in Berta that he needed and wanted. This led him to discover where she lived and to make efforts to get to know her. The next night he made a bold approach to her house.

Soon they were dating, but Berta was cautious of this ambitious young man who was a few years younger than herself. The divorce was still being finalized, but it did not deter the young entrepreneur from insisting that he loved her and wanted to marry her once she was free.

The two lonely people, he from being separated from his mother and family, and she from being separated from the man she thought she'd married for life, found mutual strength. She finally consented to marry him, quietly, in a private ceremony.

He thought about how lucky he was to marry a woman who had such strong principles, and offered so much love and support. All these thoughts flooded his mind as he embraced and kissed her on that dark porch.

"I've been worried about you, Jim. You left before dawn this morning to go down to the store and even though I took a meal down to you, I thought you'd be back before this," Berta said, trying not to show her concern with a tinge of anger.

He reached out to her, grasping her hand, as he drew a chair up beside the rocker and spoke lovingly.

"Honey, I had such an inventory to finish. I had to get it

done today before Tom Callahan came by to check things out."

"I understand," she said as she patted his hand, "but I'm concerned that you're not sleeping well. I heard you get up before dawn and rattle around in the kitchen."

"I'm sorry I disturbed you," he said, with an apologetic voice, "but I can't tell you how much I want to succeed in this store. It could mean moving up in a way that helps me to have my own chain of stores."

"Don't stop dreaming, my darling, that's why I married you—because you can see the distant stars. You can reach for them without touching them, always knowing you will come close." With this she stopped rocking and began wheezing as her asthma gripped her lungs.

He got up quickly and put his arm around her, lifted an afghan from the back of his chair and wrapped it tenderly around her.

"Ever since Tom Callahan and Guy Johnson had their dream of a chain of stores and called them 'Golden Rule Stores,' great things have been happening. It was Tom's mother, Celia Callahan, who came up with the unique idea of naming this pioneer venture The Golden Rule Stores. That wonderful woman guided those men, just as you are guiding me and supporting me. That's why I love you."

Touched by his affirmation of her role in his life, Berta looked into his eyes and said, "I do believe God led us to each other. You came to me when I was down and discouraged about marriage and I came to you when you needed other wings to help you soar to new heights."

A contented look came over Jim Penney's face as he looked skyward with an almost mystical glance and said, "Great things are happening in the merchant world. Only yesterday I heard of a man named William T. Woolworth who opened a store in Lynn, Massachusetts, called a 5 & 10 cent store. He did this because there was a need for a store with prices within the reach of the poorer people. I feel there is a place for a chain of stores between the 5 & 10 cent idea and that of the more expensive department stores."

Berta got up slowly, returned the afghan to the other chair and led her husband into the house, as she said, "Come, my beloved dreamer. Taste the beef stew I made to give you the strength to carry out that dream and then we can go to bed early."

Young Penney learned much and did so well under the tutelage of Guy Johnson and Tom Callahan that the chief partner of The Golden Rule Stores talked to Jim about going to another town and starting a new store for the chain. This would mean that J.C. Penney would become a partner in the expanding chain.

The increase in mining activities in that whole area, as well as the mounting population caused by people coming in on the busy railroad, indicated the need for more Golden Rule stores. After much deliberation and dialogue with Callahan about the best place to start next, Jim Penney convinced him that the town of Kemmerer was the most promising location.

Within a year a small building was found in Kemmerer, which had a population of 900. It had much potential for growth because of the increased activities of the Kemmerer Coal Company and other mines surrounding the area.

The frame building was remodeled and eventually stocked with merchandise from Kansas City, St. Louis, and New York City. Other goods came from Philadelphia, as well as shoes from the Massachusetts shoe mills in Lowell, Haverhill and Lynn.

Jim and Berta Penney visited the mines and distributed handbills to the workers as they emerged and headed for their homes.

The Penneys lived in a small apartment just above the store, using makeshift furniture made from the wooden boxes that arrived with goods for the store. Though the young new partner/manager kept apologizing to Berta for the flimsy and inappropriate furniture, she constantly assured him that she would be happy living in a tent on the highest snow-covered mountaintop just to be with him.

During the next year the store did well. Jim even traveled to the cities where merchandise was ordered. The latest good news was that the Penneys were due to have their first baby.

While pregnant, Berta worked as one of the sales clerks and continued to help Jim make decisions which enabled him to prove he was a wise manager and effective person. Two other people were hired to take care of the increasingly busy store.

During these busy years, Jim and Berta experienced the happiest times of their relationship. The peak day came when their first little boy was born and named Roswell; and even with the new baby Berta continued to work part-time.

Eventually the couple found a cottage on Pine Avenue across from the original store. Two years later, a second baby was born in December of 1903. He was named Johnson Callahan Penney in honor of the two men who were the helpful mentors and partners of J.C. Penney. The little boy, from that time on, was called J.C. Jr.

The sign outside the store in Kemmerer, Wyoming, read "The Golden Rule Store" and was officially tagged with the firm name of Johnson, Callahan and Penney. Some years later J.C. Penney wrote:

"The Golden Rule name was a poignant link for me with my father's and my mother's ideals and injunctions. It also reminded us of the origin of the Golden Rule which, though lifted up in the Sermon on the Mount, had been stated in the literature of eleven religions. While Christ was not the first to lift it up, He was the one to give it the most meaningful place as a perfect precept to follow in life."

The Penney philosophy of sales and management was based upon the Golden Rule as a policy which would affect all relationships within the framework of his company. It meant he was determined to show the world that a company could be run with the basic idea of making money and profit while serving the community with fair dealings and honest values.

Not only did the store at Kemmerer prosper but Guy Johnson and Tom Callahan suggested to Jim Penney that they would be open to selling their shares as partners to him so he could have sole ownership. On December 31, 1907, the young manager realized the first big act of his dream when he bought the senior partners' shares for around $30,000. The loans secured to do this were fully paid within two years. At age thirty-three, the young merchant J.C. Penney was now motivated to expand his chain of stores, with plans to establish fifty stores within the next few years.

Berta continued to give herself sacrificially while raising their boys. She also became involved in the Methodist church at Kemmerer. Meanwhile, Jim Penney sought people who were willing to learn the business and train as clerks, while being open to eventually becoming partners in The Golden Rule Stores. More new stores were founded in surrounding states. By the year 1913 there were forty-eight stores and by 1919 there were ninety-seven. In 1909 Mr. Penney gave up managing the Kemmerer store and centralized his work in Salt Lake City, Utah, where he moved Berta and the boys into a new home. He also established a warehouse and central accounting office there.

As the wife of J.C. Penney, the tireless entrepreneur, Berta talked seriously one day with her husband about becoming affiliated with a church where the boys could go to Sunday School and their parents could be spiritually fed. She did the researching and finally suggested the First Methodist Church where the Reverend Francis B. Short was the minister.

In one of the Penneys' first visits to the church to hear the Rev. Mr. Short, Jim was impressed by the imposing tall man and his forceful sermon. However, he still resisted joining the church when memories of what happened to his father in Missouri flooded his mind. He wasn't ready to make a commitment to the institution and rationalized his reluctance by convincing himself that he was not good enough to be a church member. However, Dr. Short instinctively knew what was going on and visited the Penney home many times. A strong bond of friendship was created between the clergyman and the business leader.

After ten years of struggle together, Berta and Jim decided that the time had come for them to have the honeymoon they never had when they were quietly joined together. Thus came the decision to take a trip to Europe and the Holy Land. With the addition of eight stores and the doubling of the total sales from $300,000 in 1909 to $662,300 in 1910, Jim Penney was certain that he could afford to take Berta and the boys on this belated trip. It would be their first overseas visit. They were excited about the new venture planned.

Because of her struggle with asthma, Berta was advised to have her tonsils removed before the trip. After the operation she walked from the hospital ward to their home some blocks away and was caught in a sudden December downpour. Within the week she became very ill and was diagnosed with lobar pneumonia, which in the pre-antibiotic days was a dreaded illness.

During those days before Christmas Jim Penney was checking his new stores on the Pacific Coast and making sure that all would be well there while he took the trip with Berta. A telegram came to him advising that he return immediately to Salt Lake City; his wife was running a dangerously high temperature and her lungs were full. He took the first train he could get, arriving just a few days before Christmas. He was at her side on the day after Christmas in that dark month of

1910 when her life slipped away. *Merry Christmas, Jim and boys!*

This wonderful woman had been at his side for ten years providing strength, wisdom and love. The loss was devastating! Just as he was ready to recompense her for her sacrifices and shared love she had been snatched away from him. It wasn't fair! Since 1899 she had been the mainstay of his life. Her unswerving confidence in his abilities had given him the energy and power to surmount the mountains which tried to block his progress time and time again. It was Berta who had inspired him to reach for the stars when others thought him a fool. At age thirty-five the successful business man and widowed father was crushed. How he wished his father and mother were around to help him answer the questions about God's way of dealing with him.

One great gift which Berta left for Jim was the friendship of the Rev. Dr. Short. The wonderful pastor helped to comfort, strengthen, and guide the mourning husband. But, most of all, as Penney himself wrote years later, Dr. Short provided a new perspective on "reaching for the stars."

Chapter III

The New Perspective

JAMES PENNEY SAT STRAIGHT UP IN HIS BED. HE NOTED THAT HIS pajamas were soaking wet as he reached over for Berta. She was gone! Then the reality of the dark, previous days broke in upon him like cold wind from the surrounding mountains. The death of the woman he loved was for real.

The cruel dream which had just gripped him became a replay as he sat among the rumpled bedclothes remembering the nightmare which had him in his office in Salt Lake City when his secretary handed him a telegram advising him of the bankruptcy of his stores in Kemmerer, Midvale, Bountiful and Prado. In his dream, he saw his best manager and right-hand man standing outside one of the stores, shouting at the top of his voice, and shaking his fist as he screamed, "J.C. , this is Earl Sams advising you that I'm quitting The Golden Rule Stores. I've had it with you and your self-pity because of Berta's death!"

Suddenly the scene changed to the sanctuary of the First

Methodist Church of Salt Lake City. Dr. Short stood behind his pulpit and pointed his finger at Penney shouting, "You hypocrite! You gave us money but not yourself! Berta carried the spiritual responsibilities of your family while you sold your soul to the devil in order to become a millionaire! Now your money is gone along with Berta!"

The distraught Penney struggled out of his bed and staggered toward the bathroom. The ugly dream was too real. He couldn't seem to shake its effect. The luxurious home which he'd purchased for Berta now seemed like an empty shack. He felt nauseous as he bent over the pink marble sink splashing his face with cold water.

Walking in his pajamas, while wiping his wet face and hair, he came to the top of the curved staircase bordered with walnut paneling and a wrought-iron banister. He stopped at the top step remembering how Berta had laughed with joy as the realtor led her into this luxurious area with elegant chandeliers and intricate designs painted on the soft-colored walls. He could still feel her hug as she exclaimed, "Oh, Jim, this is the realization of the dream of my life!"

Now, without Berta, the dream had changed into a nightmare! Tears began to flow down his cheeks. How could this happen? Just when he was going to take her on an overseas trip to make up for the honeymoon they never had. If only his father were here to help him come to grips with the bitterness and emptiness he felt at losing his devoted wife. He no longer felt that he had any faith in a God who would allow this to happen. All his father had taught him about the Bible and promises of God's presence and healing seemed gone. In its place was a tale of mockery.

A hand touched him tenderly, bringing him out of his dark thoughts. It was his mother who had emerged from one of the guest bedrooms and spotted her son as he stood at the top of the stairs, as though in a trance.

"Son," she whispered, trying not to wake up the boys. "What can I do for you?"

"Not a thing, Mother. I do appreciate you and Letha staying on for awhile after the funeral." He turned and hugged her close. Here was the stable, loving, supportive woman of his childhood. She and his sister, Letha, had come by train for the funeral. His mother was the one small ray of sunshine in his life that day.

"I'm sorry to have to leave you with Roswell and J.C., Jr., plus the care of this big house," he said apologetically, "but I've got to get back to some of the new stores that are opening up in our Golden Rule chain."

"Don't think a thing about it," she assured him. "Letha and I are pretty free right now and the boys can enjoy a belated Christmastime. We'll be fine. But you must take care of yourself. You are needed here. The boys need a good father."

Almost as though on signal, the two boys came running out of their bedroom. Their father knelt, receiving them with warm hugs. At this moment he needed to give his attention to the boys, even though he had to pack his suitcase for a visit to the stores outside the state.

"I'll tell you what, boys! You, Grandma, Aunt Letha and I

will make today a fun day. We're going to visit the zoo! So, get dressed warm and we'll take off after breakfast."

The boys turned and raced back to their room. Being with their father at the zoo would be a real treat. Things looked better today than they did yesterday!

Just before leaving the house, the phone rang. It was the Rev. Dr. Francis Short, inquiring of the family's condition. Jim assured him that, with mother and aunt on hand, all would be well. "I've got to take off to visit some stores tomorrow, but today I'm taking the boys to the zoo."

"That's great," responded Dr. Short, "and if I or my wife can help your mother and sister while you are away, have them phone me." Jim hung up the telephone feeling the warmth of the good will which flowed from Pastor Short.

As he walked through the garage to get his car and pick up the family, he reflected upon the happenings of the last few days. He thought of the nightmare he'd had and the caring phone call from Dr. Short. One of the major gifts that Berta had brought into their family's life was Dr. Short. It was she who had persuaded her husband to attend the church with her. When it happened the result was one of lasting benefit. James Penney was touched by the spirituality which he sensed in the pastor. Remembrances of his father came back to him but Dr. Short had a warmer, compassionate spirit. He liked him. And, as a result, the two became close friends with a bonding which blessed the years ahead.

Knowing Jim Penney's background of negative reactions to the institutional church, caused by the Hamilton church's cruel treatment of his father and mother, Pastor Short was cautiously careful not to pressure Penney to become a member of his church. However, Berta had joined the church feeling that, with time, her husband would follow. Being the type of minister who wisely knew how to wait for the seed of faith to take root in people, Dr. Short spent considerable time with Jim and the boys. He was a frequent visitor in their home and at the Penney office. He became the fragile thread of love which connected the mourning father to his God.

"How could such a thing happen to us, Dr. Short, when Berta was such a wonderful wife, mother and devoted Christian?" The agonizing question came as the pastor sat with him in the Penney kitchen sipping coffee.

"I'm not going to preach to you, Jim, but all I can say is that one important thing to remember, when we have a bad experience in life, is that it's not what happens to us that is the most significant thing but what we do with what happens to us."

The still-grieving husband just shook his head as he found he could not come up with words which expressed his feelings of desertion and loneliness. He finally attempted to tell the pastor how he felt. His loss of Berta was so devastating and his separation from God was so real.

As Dr. Short rose from the table to leave his friend, he reached over and patted his rounded shoulders and whispered, "I think I need to leave you alone, Jim, for only you can work this out. Just remember one thing—you have a heritage from Berta and your father which promises you that underneath are the everlasting arms of God. I know that sounds pretty hollow to you right now, but praying will help you to come through. Even if you don't feel like praying I want you to know that I will be on my knees daily on your behalf. Don't forget that."

With this final word the pastor slipped out the back door leaving Jim Penney to contemplate on what he had tried to communicate.

In spite of the efforts of Dr. Short, Jim's mother, and other friends, the agonizing J.C. Penney kept sinking deeper and deeper into the pit of despair. Though he had grown up with an abhorrence of alcoholic drinking, he found himself drawn in the direction of drinking as a means of drowning his sorrows. He even shared later in life his contemplated suicide efforts but the image of the praying Dr. Short kept him from that.

The demands of his business required trips to New York City where he spent many sleepless nights, walking the streets, trying to find some way to get back to normal. His efforts at praying were useless.

On one cold snowy January night, he left his hotel room to walk to the Bowery. Perhaps he unconsciously felt that that was the place where the "down and outers" were and he belonged among them.

As he went down a Bowery street, he heard singing which drew him toward the open door of a mission. A blinking sign and large lighted cross hung on the front of the mission. The music he heard was familiar. Some men were singing, "Jesus Lover of My Soul," which happened to be his mother's favorite hymn. He entered the mission and saw a group of men; most were unshaven, unkempt, dirty and smelly. They were typical street people, sitting and singing in a place that gave them warmth, food and friendliness on that bitter cold winter night. The leader stood behind a pulpit, waving his arms to lead the group, which seemed most uncomfortable with the old traditional hymn. Each of the men, Penney noted, looked as bad as he felt.

After reading from the Bible, and leading a prayer, the mission leader introduced a well-dressed man who told those present that not too long before he had sat where they were sitting and someone spoke that night in such a way that God came into his life.

Penney sat transfixed as he heard this man tell how far down he had gone after the loss of a loved one and the loss of his job. He reminded the listeners, some of whom had fallen asleep, that man's extremities were God's opportunities. He told how he had tried to run away from God but the Father had reached down and touched him. He was reflecting the peace and the joy that had changed his life.

Back in the hotel Jim reflected upon what he had heard that night. He remembered the Bible story of the Prodigal Son which had often been used as the basis of his father's sermons. He felt that God had led him to that mission where, at the close of the service, he had pressed a check into the hand of the mission leader. He made a decision to give up the idea of drinking and to make a move in a direction which would give him a new perspective.

Returning to Salt Lake City, he shared with Dr. Short what had happened at the mission. He pledged a closer relationship with the church, but was still not yet ready to join it. He offered to be more generous in his financial support of the church as an expression of his gratitude to God for what had happened in his business. This was the beginning of his new venture as a philanthropic giver. Within a year he had talked with his friend, the pastor, and given $10,000 to pay off the church mortgage while memorializing Berta.

Penney also sought out Earl Corda Sams, who was his best manager and partner in The Golden Rule Stores. He shared his New York experience with him and indicated he was ready to make some significant changes in the business management of their stores. The two men were becoming closer in every way. Mr. Sams wrote to a friend and said, "James Cash Penney is one of the best businessmen I've ever met. I think more of him each day we work together." Shortly after, Penney made Mr. Sams his vice president and later he became president of the corporation.

Earl Sams helped the renewed James Penney to change The Golden Rule Stores to the J.C. Penney Corporation. Together they decided to centralize the store chain in New York City and change its structure from partnerships to incorporation. They reaffirmed the principle of partnership among the employees of the company in carrying out the philosophy of the Golden Rule as a basic guide in customer relations.

Totally immersed in the new J.C. Penney Corporation, Mr. Penney kept in close touch with Dr. Short while attending worship during his times at home. He made sure that Roswell and J.C. Jr. attended the church school. He wanted them to have the moral and spiritual enhancement that Berta would have wanted.

Eventually he began to think of the aborted honeymoon trip he had been planning to take with Berta. Believing that she would want him to still have that overseas journey, he went to Dr. Short proposing that the pastor accompany him and the two boys on such a trip. With help from the pastor, plans were made. As Penney told some other friends, it was all a desire he had to continue his search for the meaning of life. It was one more phase in his spiritual journey.

The group left by ship and headed for Europe, Egypt, Palestine and the Holy Land. Some other business acquaintances accompanied the group. Dr. Short became the guide who shared his scholarly knowledge and universal insights. Still being careful not to give the impression that he was trying to convert Penney, the wise pastor had continued using opportunities to open up Penney's mind and reach into his soul.

The worn-out, depressed Penney began to show signs of renewal of body, mind and spirit. As he shared with Dr. Short, on one of their last days journeying, "I've found I can't run away from God. What has happened to me these last two years have done just what you predicted. I'm ready to go home as a new person and begin all over again. But now I have my feet on solid ground. I guess walking where Jesus walked helped me to come to that conclusion."

One of the things that made Penney ponder the matter of fate was that for the return trip the group was supposed to go to Liverpool and board the Titanic for its second trip at sea. Word came to them, while they were touring Europe, that the Titanic, on its maiden voyage, had struck an iceberg and 1517 lives had been lost!

The learning experiences for J.C. Penney during this journey helped him make major changes in his lifestyle, his business and in his social relationships. He returned to the States with his soul recharged with a new power. He would share his money with significant projects. He had a new sense of mission as a pioneer in marketing. He came back with a new appreciation of life in the United States. He arrived with a new vision concerning the long-range potential of the J.C. Penney Corporation. Berta would have been very happy. It was all worthwhile.

CHAPTER IV

REDISCOVERING LOVE

JIM PENNEY KNOCKED ON AN OFFICE DOOR WITH A PLAQUE ON IT
which read, "EARL SAMS, PRESIDENT." A cheerful voice
said, "Come in, whoever you are."

The intruder pushed open the door and peered in,
observing that Mr. Sams was on the telephone. While the new
Penney Corporation President finished his call, with a welcoming gesture he urged the recently elevated Chairman of
the Board Penney to sit in the new leather chair in front of his
desk.

As the phone call continued, Jim Penney studied the busy
executive, thinking how much Sams had meant to him and
how he had proven to be his strongest helper since leaving
Kansas so many years before and joining the growing Penney
venture in Colorado.

He thought of how far they had come in setting up their
offices in New York City. He also reflected upon the decision
he'd made to retire as president of the thriving business, with

the hope of rebuilding his life and spirit since returning from his trip to Europe and the Holy Land. Earl Sams had been a gift from God and J.C. Penney had offered many a prayer of gratitude for the steadfastness and business acumen of the partner.

Hanging up the phone, Earl looked into the eyes of his boss and noticed a sparkle which signaled that something new was in the wind.

"Seems like you have some good news for me, Jim. Something positive has happened in our victory over Germany or are you already planning on twenty-five more stores?"

"Who knows, Earl? Things are going well in spite of the consequences of the war or, perhaps I should say, because of the war. Actually we've been confident that President Wilson would lead us to some new heights. We've already received a tremendous economic boost because of our new clothes styles and because our prices are good for people feeling the pinch of the hard times caused by the war." Then he hesitated and looked out the window overlooking New York City as though he was searching for words.

Sensing that this visit was different, Earl Sams got up from his chair, went around the desk and sat next to Penney. "Well, then, out with it...do we have a problem I didn't know about?"

"No, things are going well, but I have an announcement to make which might surprise you."

"Nothing you would do would surprise me, Jim. I've always related to you through the years as one expecting something new and exciting every week."

"But this is different. It doesn't concern the company. It's personal. You'll remember that on my life-changing trip overseas, something happened to me and I came back a new man."

"How well I remember. All of us noticed how much it had helped you to find new energies and new spirit."

"It's turned out to be more than that," said Penney, as he reached into his suitcoat pocket and pulled out a picture. He handed it to Sams and the president studied it thoughtfully.

"That's Mary Hortense Kimball. We were introduced by Dr. Short during our return trip on the ship back to New York. She had been working for the Red Cross in France."

"I remember you telling me about her." Sams handed the photo back to Penney and added, "She's pretty."

"She's more than pretty; she's smart, mature and deeply spiritual. We corresponded until she returned to Utah where I've had opportunities to visit her."

"So that's why you've been making so many trips to Utah these days. And here I thought it was to check out our stores," Sams said laughingly.

Penney got up from his chair and stood by the window. Turning to Sams, with seriousness he said, "I'm going to marry her. We've discovered we're in love and that's something I thought would never happen since losing Berta."

"Some of us were hoping that would happen because we know how lonely you've been and how you've struggled to provide a home for the boys."

"Yes, and she has the education I never had. She graduated from Bryn Mawr where she majored in French and music and studied in Paris. She has the cultural and international viewpoint I discovered on my trip. Every time I'm with her she awakens desires within me to grow in mind and spirit."

"Sounds tremendous!" exclaimed Earl Sams, as he sprang from his chair and grasped the hand of the man who meant so much to him. "Congratulations! When's the big day?"

"We've agreed upon July 29th and we'll be joined together as husband and wife at her parents' home in Salt Lake City."

The wedding was a gala event with family and Penney Corporation executives invited to the reception.

The bride and groom returned to New York and Jim took his bride to "White Haven," the lovely fifty-acre estate he had purchased in White Plains, just twenty miles from his office in New York City.

Everyone surrounding Jim Penney saw him as a new person. The appointment of Earl Sams as president lifted a great burden from his shoulders. The arrival of Dr. Short as the new educational director of the company provided a spiritual mentor for Penney. The new efforts by him to seek tutoring in public speaking and improvement in the skills of communication all seemed to be pieces of the Penney puzzle being set in place, with Mary as the key piece to bring it all together in creating a renewed man.

Freed up by new opportunities to retreat from the cold winters of New York, the next thing Jim did was take his new bride to Florida where he had discovered its warm benefits for the health of the family.

Jim and Mary arrived in Miami by train and were met by

a taxi which took them to Belle Isle, a small off-shore paradise, which was one of several islands connected by a causeway across the Biscayne Bay.

This area had been discovered and improved by the northern wealthy who poured money into the Miami surroundings, transforming mud flats into semi-tropical gardens.

As the two approached Belle Isle, Jim took hold of Mary's hand and said, "Ever since I came here over five years ago, I've wanted to have a place to come to for the December until May months.

"You'll see," he said, as he pointed out some homes to Mary, "that these are not the super-luxury estates like those owned by the Fords and Vanderbilts, but it's a far cry from my background in Missouri. In fact, the place I've bought for you is a typical Penney product, nice but not luxurious."

Mary laughed as she squeezed his hand. "Jim, you don't have to apologize for not spending your money to impress others. That's why I love you." She leaned over and kissed him on the check, just as they approached the newly purchased home.

As the brilliant Florida sun reflected off the white-walled, two-story house with its apricot tiled roof, Mary thought of the Italian Renaissance homes she'd seen in Capri. Riding up to a huge wrought-iron gate, Mary gasped as she watched an expectant caretaker open the gate wide. The car entered and drove down a driveway lined with palm trees. She saw Spanish stopper bushes planted around the house, and gardens were located all over the property. Some were ablaze with various colored roses. Others had morning glories in full bloom and patches of dwarf lantana. Zephyr lilies provided a white background for the rainbow of tropical colors. The sight was breathtaking.

Her husband didn't say a word as he watched the emotions of his pleased wife. It took him back to the first time he took Berta into the little cottage they had rented on Pine Avenue in Kemmerer.

Once inside the newly furnished house the couple stood in silent wonder as they studied the huge living room with its high cathedral ceiling and beautiful Italian Renaissance lines.

"Well," asked Jim, as he put his arm around Mary, "do you like it?"

"I'm speechless, Jim. I never dreamed it would be so perfect." Then she went over to the large arched windows overlooking the azure ocean. "And though I've been all over the world with my parents, this is the loveliest scene of all—because I'm with you—the man of my dreams."

"Come see the other rooms," he urged, as though a little overwhelmed by the sentiments of his wife. He led her into the music room which had handwoven carpets, antique furniture pieces and flowers in large vases. In one corner was a huge organ and in the other a Steinway grand piano.

"It's almost too much to grasp. I feel like a little girl who's at the Christmas tree finding everything she ever asked Santa for." With this she sat at the piano and gently played their wedding song, "I Love You Truly."

Jim Penney thought about God and how he had been led from those struggling days in Denver to this high point in his life. Dr. Short had assured him at his wedding to Mary that the best days were still ahead. And everything seemed to say his spiritual advisor was right again.

Many joyous experiences would be enjoyed at Belle Isle. Mary proved to be the perfect hostess. She and her husband entertained Herbert Hoover, William Jennings Bryant, William Vanderbilt, Andrew Carnegie and others. Mary utilized her musical background to invite notable musicians like Arthur Rubenstein to play for guests in their winter home.

Writers in the local newspapers pointed out that J.C. Penney's winter home was more modest than those of other millionaires in the Miami region.

Mark Twain would have said, "J. C. Penney avoided the gilded-age style of life."

When the couple returned to White Plains to be reunited with Roswell and J.C. Jr., who had been cared for through the months by sister Letha, the man who a Miami newspaper called, "The Most Modest Millionaire," got back into the swing of things.

He visited colleges with Roswell who was leaning towards Princeton. He spent time with Sams catching up on things at the office. Stores were being added to their company and more than fifty million dollars worth of business was being enjoyed.

Jim Penney even took time to visit J.C. Jr. who was in a prep school nearby. He took Mary's advice and tried to build new bridges between himself and the boys.

Then, on September 28, 1920, Mary Kimball Penney presented her proud husband with a new baby boy, whom they named Kimball. This brought a whole new change of lifestyle to White Haven and Belle Isle. The dynamic merchant was thrust into a new role along with his attempts at finding more time for meditation and prayer.

Regular coffee appointments with Dr. Short continued, as the patient and wise spiritual advisor continued to mold the friend who had bonded with him those years previously.

At the same time the former farmer-boy began planting gardens on his acreage at White Haven. Even as he had rediscovered love in Mary Kimball, he rediscovered the love of the land, the feel of dirt on his hands, and the fulfillment which he knew as a boy in seeing the wonders of nature's productivity.

Little by little he added chickens, sheep and pigs to this New York estate, much to the surprise of their nearest neighbors. Much later this land would be taken over by the city and used as a school building location.

During this rediscovery process, two things happened which caused Penney to go to his knees. The first was the unexpected death of his sister, Pearl Penney Strawn, who died in childbirth in her home in Oregon. The shock of Pearl's death shook her brother tremendously. They had been very close while growing up in Missouri.

The second blow to Penney happened while he was with Mary and Kimball at their favorite retreat spot at Belle Isle.

His wife became violently ill. Several doctors were rushed to her side and discovered she was bleeding internally. She soon was unconscious with extreme abdominal pain. The consulting doctors talked about rushing her to the Miami hospital for possible surgery. They discussed this with her husband but convinced him that going to the hospital might not save her.

Not too many hours later, Mary Kimball Penney breathed her last while her weeping husband stayed at her side. He couldn't believe this was really happening to him all over again. The darkness of Berta's death, then Pearl's and now this wonderful woman who had given him such love for three and a half years, had begun to engulf him again.

That night he knelt by his empty bed and prayed in an anguished voice, "Oh, God, how often I've prayed to You since my father's death. I've searched for You and still have not found You! You took my hand when Berta died and then you gave me Mary's hand. I'd found a new love and it's all gone from me so swiftly!

"Forgive me, Father, for doubting You. But, how could I lose two whom I loved so much? Where are You, Lord! I need You! Help me!"

He rose from his knees and, as he slipped between the cool sheets, he seemed to hear his father's voice, just as he'd heard it so many times from his pulpit, "I will not leave you comfortless, I will come to you."

These words of Jesus had been spoken to him many times by Dr. Short. He was not alone! He was surrounded by those who reminded him of God's love. God had given him Mary and baby Kimball. Life would be different from here on.

He slept in peace. He had bigger things to do! They would be dedicated to Mary Kimball Penney who had brought a sunshine to his life symbolized by Belle Isle.

Chapter V

The Last Frontier

He sat on the wooden dock, in his shirtsleeves, his tie and coat at his side, with his feet dangling over the front of the dock. Rarely would anyone see J.C. Penney with his coat and tie off, but it was very hot in Green Cove Springs, Florida.

The St. Johns River fascinated the native of Missouri. As he watched, a passenger steamer loaded with waving passengers and a tugboat pulling a barge in the opposite direction came into view. He thought of the times his father had taken him to the Missouri River and how he dreamed about what it was like where those boats were heading. Perhaps they were going to unexplored regions.

He breathed deeply of the warm, clear air and found renewal in just being by himself. Though mosquitoes landed on his face and bare arms, he did not mind their intrusion. He was praying, asking for God's leading in this important visit to that town of northern Florida. He was also thanking God for Berta, Dr. Short, and Mary Kimball, for their urging him to find a closer relationship with God. His visit to Green Cove Springs was directly related to their admonitions to help other people.

Just before her sudden death, Mary had made a large contribution to an orphanage in Salt Lake City and she talked extensively to her husband about it. Every time he stopped to reflect and pray, her act and words she had shared with him about this memorial to her mother kept coming back.

With these things crowding his mind, James Penney drank in the tranquil beauty of the blue waters sparkling in the bright sun.

Suddenly, a voice spoke to him. He was startled out of his reverie, as he turned to see a rather shabbily-dressed man sitting down next to him.

"Good mornin', suh, nice day," the stranger said in a low, gruff voice, as he opened a can of worms and began to bait the fishing line on the bamboo pole.

Penney studied him for a few moments and then decided to be courteous and make a reply.

"Yes, it is nice. A lot warmer than where I come from."

"I take it you're visiting our famous pool. Where you from?"

"I've just arrived from New York City for business purposes." He decided he would not share with this stranger the specific reason for his visit.

"Well," said the stranger, as he offered his dirty hand to the visitor. "I'm Zeke Hill and I live here. I come down to the dock to fish every break I get."

Penney shook the extended hand and said, "You must know an awful lot about this area."

"Know it pretty well," he grunted, as he dropped his line in the water. "I should, my family goes way back to the Indians. My daddy says I have Seminole blood in me." Then he added, "We've always lived near this river. That's why the Indians came here in the first place. I just worship the old St. Johns."

Some moments passed while Zeke relocated his line and Penney thought about the use of the word "worship."

"Do you know that this great river flows from south to north?" asked Zeke. "One of the few in the world to do that. Some brochures up at the hotels call it the 'Nile of the South.' I ain't never been to the real Nile...guess it's pretty nice."

"From what I've heard the Nile is dirty. But I don't think I know where this river originates."

"It begins in the marshes and springs of Brevard County, 260 miles south of here, and flows 20 miles inland off the East Coast. Ends up in Mayport just 30 miles east of Jacksonville."

Zeke jerked up his line and Penney saw he had caught what appeared to be a good-sized catfish. Then, when he slammed the catfish on the dock to stun it for unhooking, he also splattered water and blood all over Mr. Penney, who jumped to his feet.

While watching the fisherman take the fish off the hook, J.C. decided to ask some more questions of this man who seemed more knowledgeable than his dress or speech would indicate.

"Tell me something about Clay County. I know it's

become quite a tourist center here in Green Cove Springs because of the warm springs."

"Yup, we've seen the railroad put through here on the way to Miami, seen the hotels built, seen the nice restaurants which we can't afford to eat in, seen the lumber mills opened up and seen 'em close down after they stripped a lot of our forests."

"Are there any Seminoles still around?" Penney asked

"Hardly any, they was scattered, pushed out, carried out. And my Granddaddy told me how sad it was. The only ones stayin' here were those who married whites. That's how it happened to my family."

"I imagine your granddad had lots to tell you about the old days here."

"Yup. Tole me about the paddle wheelers—that was the only way you could come in here before the trains. Used to go up Black Creek to Middleboro when the whites first settled."

"And eventually the lumber people came in and set up mills and shops to make things out of the pine wood?"

"Yup," said Zeke as he began to bring in his line and put the top on his bait can, "but even though the lumber business finally shut down, the warm springs saved us. But the best thing of all was when Mr. Frank Gustafson opened the first Ford dealership in the State of Florida right here in Green Cove Springs."

"I've noticed," said Penney, "a lot of Fords and even some roads paved to go in and out of here."

"Yup," exclaimed Zeke as he gathered up his things to leave, "and I got a job in the Ford garage. That's where I been when I came down here on my lunch break. I'm doin' cleanup there but I'm learning to be a mechanic."

Penney thanked the Ford worker for his information, picked up his coat and tie, and sauntered toward the Qui-Si-Sana Hotel (Here is Health Hotel). Passing the reservoir filled with splashing visitors, he paused to watch them play in the mineral waters now bubbling in the large pool. No wonder they called this place "The Watering Hole" of the rich.

His mind went back to a book he'd read which told of the discoverer Jean Ribault, a commander of French Huguenots who, when he landed on this shore off the St. Johns River wrote, "This is the fairest, fruitfulest, and pleasantest place in the whole world."

With all the rush by speculators to buy up the land for sale in southern Florida, J.C. Penney was certain that the safest investment would be in the northern area where the vast pine forests could be utilized with little need for special attention and expense. He also felt that though there were lakes, rivers, and some swamps in the Clay County region, they would be at a higher and dryer elevation than what he'd seen around Belle Isle.

On one of his train trips through this county, while on his way southward, a conductor on his sleeper once said, "Land is cheap out there," as he pointed out at the pine forests through which their train puffed its way. "Only recently I heard of a man who traded 100 acres of his land as a swap for a hunting hound dog! I wish I had the money to buy some of it. I'd become a millionaire!"

The thought of buying some of that land merged with the

advice of Dr. Short to Penney about giving more to help others. Perhaps, he thought, *God will open the door to my dream of doing something in memory of my former clergyman father and my saintly mother.*

Later, Penney shared with Earl Sams the possibility of doing something in northern Florida which would not be for speculation or profit but as an investment in human lives. He specified that he was especially interested in helping struggling farmers and retired clergy.

Then someone had informed him of an ad in a New York paper which told of 120,000 acres that were for sale in Clay County where Green Cove Springs was the town which served as the county seat. This was the reason he had come to the "Water Hole of the Wealthy."

Back at the hotel Mr. Penney called the Clay County Courthouse to inquire about the 120,000 acres that were for sale. He was informed by the County Clerk that the Clay County circuit court was responsible for a public auction of the land and buildings owned by the Florida Farms and Industries Co. They had fallen upon bad times and were placed in receivership. A ruling had been made that the property they held would be sold shortly, at an announced public auction.

With the news of this coming sale, Penney rushed back to his office in New York and had a meeting with some of his top colleagues in the corporation. Out of this came a new corporation formed with the help of Ralph W. Gwinn, who had joined Penney in the 1920 activities. Gwinn and Penney became the co-directors of the J.C. Penney-Gwinn

Corporation, a separate entity from the J.C. Penney Corporation.

This new corporation was brought into being in order to carry out Penney's personal business ventures and his philanthropic activities. At the same time the J.C. Penney Foundation was also formed. The first big steps toward helping others had been taken.

Mr. Gwinn returned to Green Cove Springs with Penney and they appeared at the scheduled auction where they submitted a bid for $400,000. This was accepted on February 24, 1925. One more step had been taken in the "last frontier" toward the goal of carrying out the Penney dream. The 120,000 acres purchased covered one-third of the tree-covered Clay County, reached twenty-eight miles southwest of Jacksonville, and even included the Qui-Si-Sana Hotel where he had first stayed in that county. This also included the purchase of the former Dowling-Shands Lumber Company which had some buildings and cottages located on the banks of the St. Johns River.

Two things happened prior to the acquisition of the acreage in Florida which were significant. First, the 500th J.C. Penney store was opened in Hamilton, Missouri. The very building where Jim Penney first entered the dry-goods business world in 1895 was for sale. Mr. J.M. Hale had announced his plan to retire and his desire to sell his store. This prompted J.C. Penney to visit the man who had offered him the first opportunity to learn the business which he grew to love.

Sitting with his old friend, Penney said, "Mr. Hale, I could have sent Earl Sams to negotiate with you about buying this property, but you gave me my first break when I was just a poor farmer boy."

Mr. Hale leaned forward and looked into the eyes of this famous merchant-millionaire and said, with a catch in his voice, "Jim...little did I ever realize that you would rise to such heights."

Penney looked a little embarrassed as he said, "Sir, I did not do this alone. God was with me more than I knew, and my wives were part of it all, along with the wonderful partners who eventually joined me."

"I've wondered with all your achievements, and seeing the large number of stores you've opened, even in Missouri, why you didn't come to Hamilton sooner? Since this is the place where you were born and raised, I would think that you would have started a store here a long time ago. Everyone in town was sure you'd come here and force me to retire earlier."

"All I can say, Mr. Hale, is that we weren't ready for that yet." He paused, thinking of the many times the people at the New York office had urged him to move into Hamilton and put in a new Penney store. He refused to allow that to happen, reminding his colleagues that it was J.M. Hale who set him on his adventuresome course.

"He deserves more than being put out of business," the Penney president had said, "I will wait until he makes a move which allows me to buy him out and put my name on that store. Then it will be the only Penney store in town—not a cheap competitor!"

A mutual agreement between the two men resulted in the

500th Penney store in Hamilton and the dignified, happy retirement of J.M. Hale.

The second thing that happened to J.C. Penney at this stage in his life was his becoming acquainted with Dr. Daniel A. Poling, then the senior minister of the famous Marble Collegiate Church on Fifth Avenue, New York City.

He met him at a meeting of Temperance Society people in New York. The business mogul was greatly impressed by Dr. Poling. He was physically attractive, had a melodious voice, and an aura of charisma. Poling reminded him of Dr. Short. He sensed Poling was also a man of influencing spiritual power. There was an immediate rapport between them.

The New York pastor did what almost any minister would have done, especially in meeting a man of Penney's reputation and discovering that he had no specific church affiliation; he invited him to one of his services at Marble Collegiate Church.

Penney went to a Sunday worship service. While meditating and praying during the organ prelude, he thought, *God has probably led me to this man just as He led me to Dr. Short. It's obvious that God doesn't just drop plans into my lap. He leads me to people who can help me find my purpose in life. Now, another person has entered my life who can be the latest answer to my personal needs, as well as the needs of the Penney Corporation.*

At the close of the service, the visiting Penney invited Dr. and Mrs. Poling to dine with him in a well-known restaurant on Fifth Avenue. As they sat together at a table in the corner of the restaurant, Penney asked Poling about his involvement in the International Christian Endeavor Society. Soon to be the president of that immense ecumenical youth movement, the pastor shared the story of his life and how he had come to Marble Collegiate Church, as well as become the head of the Christian Endeavor Society.

After this first meeting, J.C. Penney felt that Daniel Poling might be just the person he was looking for to help operate the carefully designed foundation which he had brought into being.

Later, Penney met with Dr. Poling when they both attended a meeting of "The Committee of One Thousand" which was created for the purpose of supporting the 18th amendment and the Volstead Act. Out of this came Poling's involvement in the Penney-Gwinn Corporation and the Penney Foundation which was about to carry out plans for the use of the land purchased in Clay County.

Florida's "last frontier" was about to experience one of the most fascinating and unique ventures in U.S. history. J.C. Penney, with great persons on his team and believing the hand of God was guiding him, was about to enter an era of experimentation which would influence the entire country.

CHAPTER VI

BACK TO THE FARM

MORE THAN FOUR HUNDRED PEOPLE SAT AROUND THE FESTIVELY decorated tables in the elegant ballroom of the Qui-Si-Sana Hotel on a cold February day in 1927.

Discussions were taking place about President Calvin Coolidge and whether he was or was not providing leadership for the country. Some were telling of their visits to the latest talking movies and the sensations they were causing. Others were complaining about the new price of the latest Ford car, which was up to $495.00. Since the average income in the United States was $2,400.00 and even a loaf of bread cost $.09, most of those present were glad they had chosen farming as their new wave of the future.

Suddenly, there was an interruption of the cacophony of voices as the crowd, composed of men, women and young people, saw something happening at the guest table. A hush fell over the cavernous hall as a distinguished gray-haired man with black suit, starched white shirt, and fancy bow tie was ushered to a seat at the center of the table.

"It's Mr. Penney!" someone at the back of the hall shouted. As if on signal, everyone leaped to their feet and began clapping and cheering. The thunderous applause continued like the rolling of kettledrums drawing attention to the crescendo of a thrilling symphony.

"Please!" shouted Mr. Clark, the chairman of the gathering as he pounded his soup spoon on the table. "Please, let's have it quiet while Mr. Penney takes his seat!" But the clapping and stomping of feet continued.

Mr. Penney stood at his place at the table and waved vigorously to the welcoming crowd, with a big smile on his tanned face. That did it. They stopped their applause and sat in their seats.

"This is a tremendous occasion for all of us," the chairman said with loud enthusiasm. "For we're here to celebrate the second anniversary of the Penney-Gwinn Corporation Farms of Clay County, Florida!"

Again the people there broke into applause, mixed with whistles and stomping of feet. Mr. Penney waved to them from his seat.

Mr. Clark introduced the guests at the head table and then called on Dr. Daniel Poling, of Philadelphia, to open the occasion with a prayer of thanksgiving. Immediately following this, as the hungry farmers and their families reached for the food before them, four men appeared from a side door. Their neighbors and friends laughed and clapped as they recognized them as fellow farmers.

"We hoe, we hoe, we hoe," they sang. Dressed in coveralls,

wearing straw hats, with shovels over their shoulders, they danced to the rhythm of a small band located behind the guest table. Their song, written by one of their wives, was all about those present arriving at the new farm community two years before. They sang of the new experiences, the dignity of farming, the joy among families in the exciting venture of moving to Florida, and the gratitude they felt for Mr. J.C. Penney who had made it all possible.

The entertainment set an upbeat mood of excitement which was reinforced when a number of waiters appeared, carrying trays loaded with food to be added to what was already on the tables.

John Snowhook, a reporter from *The Manufacturing Record*, a magazine of Baltimore, Maryland, was seated next to a couple who had two children with them. The reporter introduced himself and inquired about their presence at the anniversary banquet.

"We're the Boyles family," said the handsome, thirty-year-old farmer, as he shook the reporter's hand, gripping it so that the reporter winced at his strength. "This is my wife, Ruby, and our two boys, Jeremiah and Samuel. I'm Harry, and we've been here about six months. Came by train from Nebraska. It's wonderful to meet you. Are you one of us?"

"Well, no, I'm from a magazine in Baltimore that's read by farmers. We heard about the Institute of Applied Agriculture which Mr. Penney founded and decided to visit here."

"That's wonderful," exclaimed Ruby Boyles, as she passed a platter of meat to the reporter. "There are a number of other reporters who are here for the same reason. I guess the exciting news of this unique experiment is causing national attention."

"Not only national, but international," Mr. Snowhook responded. "I met a man on the train who came all the way from Sweden. Maybe he was like me. It wasn't just the story I was looking for but an excuse for escaping the icy, snowy weather of Baltimore."

"I miss my skiing," said little Samuel as he joined the dialogue.

"How did you happen to come here as a family?" asked the reporter as he put other foods on his plate. "You came all the way from Nebraska to this new development? Wasn't it pretty risky?"

"Well," answered Harry, "I have a cousin who used to live in Middleburg, Florida. He told us about the farming experiment here in Long Branch, and what Mr. Penney had done in starting the Institute and building the farmhouses for farmers who wanted to begin over again. I applied through the J.C. Penney store in our town and here we are."

While the waiters added still more food to the tables, young Jeremiah reached for something and accidentally knocked over a pitcher of milk which began moving down the table like a threatening flood tide.

The parents leaped quickly to their feet attempting to stop the milk from engulfing the reporter and other guests at the table.

"Oh, Jeremiah! Haven't we lectured you enough about waiting until you've been served?" scolded his mother. She reached for the embarrassed boy and urged him to swap places with his younger brother, so he would be sitting next to his stern-faced father.

Samuel smirked gleefully at his older brother's being in trouble. Usually it was the other way around.

"You always told us, Mom, not to cry over spilt milk, and besides, it's from our cows, and there's plenty more where that came from."

Mr. Snowhook could see that the parents were not too thrilled with Samuel's attempt at being cute.

"Hey," said the reporter, as he helped the parents wipe up the milk. "This just makes me feel at home. I'm a dad, two boys and a girl, and I didn't expect to see so many young people and children here."

"What did you expect?" asked Harry, obviously hoping to direct attention to something other than their family.

"Well, I didn't expect to see so many children."

"Over ninety families have come to be a part of this farm project in the last year and a half," explained Ruby, as she nudged Jeremiah who began to reach for a second piece of pie.

"I'm amazed at how this project seems to be growing. I came, primarily, to visit the Agricultural Institute, but I haven't seen the farms of Long Branch yet."

"Ya oughta come visit us and see my new calf," interjected Jeremiah as he looked quizzically at his mother and father to see if he was making another mistake.

"Oh, yes," Ruby added warmly, "we'd love to have you see our little farm. We're very proud of what's happening there."

"I can't figure out how you can do anything with the sandy, desert-like soil you live on. My boss is especially anxious to know whether all this is for real or just another Florida land speculation scam."

Harry Boyles stiffened at the suggestion of a farm scam and said, "The only one who could be scammed is Mr. Penney. We're not paying anything for the land or the house, except a small rental fee. In fact the tools, animals, and leadership are all made possible through the Penney-Gwinn Corporation at a ridiculously low price during the first year."

At that point in the conversation Mr. Clark, who Mr. Snowhook of Baltimore learned from the programs passed around was the Farm Manager, banged on the table advising people that the program was about to begin.

"We do have some speakers here," he said, as he mopped his brow with the cloth napkin in his hand, "and we have many visitors who came to learn about what's happening here. One thing that just happened is the vote of the Town Council to rename Long Branch to Penney Farms." At this the audience applauded. He went on, "And we are so fortunate to have Mr. Penney with us. Sir, will you say a few words? After all you're the one who started all this."

Looking a little embarrassed, J.C. Penney dabbed his mustache with his napkin, slowly folded it and rose to his feet, saluting the people as they clapped loudly once again.

"I thank you, Mr. Clark, for this auspicious occasion and for the warm welcome. We've come a long way in two years, and I've come a long way, with God's help.

"My wife regrets she couldn't be here with me. She's

home caring for our new baby girl." The applause began again. He continued, "I want to pay tribute to Caroline Bertha Autenreith whom I was so fortunate to marry over a year ago. She is such a wonderfully sympathetic and supportive wife who has helped in making me a bigger and better person. Through her steadfastness and projection of her religious faith, as well as her unquestioning depth concerning people and world needs, I have been spiritually charged and I feel so blessed." Then he added, with a twinkle in his eyes, "I'm sorry most of you missed the wedding in Paris." The crowd laughed.

He went on, "I know there are those who are skeptical about this project on behalf of the small farmer, but I would remind you all that I began on a small farm and the farm is still in me.

"In spite of the existence of eight hundred thriving Penney stores, I'm coming more and more to the conclusion that money and success is not enough to help one discover the deeper meaning of life." He paused as though searching for words, then went on, "My father, my father's farm and my father's faith are all linked together, for in my father's life I saw the connection between the land and the Lord. Not all at once—it's taken me to this middle period in my life to realize the place of the Lord, thanks to people like my wife, Dr. Poling, Attorney Ralph Gwinn and others who are sitting at this table today. Leaders like Dr. Johnson, who heads the Institute, and Mr. Clark, who manages the farms, gave up secure teaching positions to join me in risk-taking, in faith-venturing."

At this point in his speech, Mrs. Boyles leaned over to her husband and whispered, "For all his talk about the Lord and spirituality, he still doesn't belong to any church and he hasn't even been baptized."

Her husband put his finger to his lips, fearing that others might hear her.

Other speakers followed Mr. Penney, while the Boyles children fidgeted impatiently. They were pleased when a break came in the speech-making and fiddlers and trumpeters livened up the meeting with what seemed to be Florida "hoe-down" music. Then, at 10:30 P.M., much to the disgust of the children, one more speaker was introduced.

Dr. Albert A. Johnson, former head of the Farmingdale School of Agriculture in New York, and president of the J.C. Penney-Gwinn Institute of Applied Agriculture spoke. He reminded people of the purpose of the Institute which was established primarily for eighteen-year-olds and over who wanted to make agriculture their life vocation. He informed them of the classes available and the intern compensation plan in effect. He reminded them of the Penney model, which was partnership offering the potential of becoming farm managers after diligent application.

He went on to describe the detailed soil survey being made of the entire 120,000 acres by U.S. Government specialists and the Department of Agronomy of the Institute.

In his conclusion, which was welcomed by sighs of relief from all the children present, he said, "And let me remind you that it is the magnanimous spirit of Mr. Penney and his associates that has made these opportunities possible. Only his and their great faith in God, in Florida, and all mankind, makes our present successes possible. Thus we are assured of the wonderful future facing Penney Farms!"

After a benediction the people began to leave the hall while John Snowhook expressed his gratitude to the Boyles family for sitting with him.

"May I take you up on the invitation to visit you? At least as it came through Jeremiah?"

Without hesitation Harry Boyles patted the reporter on the shoulder and said, "Sure, there's a train that goes out of here every morning to Penney Farms." Then looking at his wife for approval he added, "I think you can get there just about the time we're finishing our morning chores."

His wife shrugged her shoulders in a kind of semi-approval and the boys chimed in, "And you can see our new calf!" And Samuel added, "And you can see my hens which have already won prizes at the Jacksonville Fair!"

CHAPTER VII

THE VISIT

THE OLD BLACK ENGINE PUFFED OUT BLACK SMOKE AND GROUND rhythmically as it tugged and pulled the few coaches and freight cars up the slope, west of Green Cove Springs, on the way to Penney Farms.

As they stopped at Pierce Station, John Snowhook squinted his eyes as he looked out the window into the brilliance of the low winter sun. He saw little wooden homes where, apparently, blacks lived just east of Penney Farms. One lady was hanging out her wash on a line strung between two pine trees while a little boy played in the sand at her feet. Then the train, with whistle blowing, approached rows of farmhouses with gardens surrounding them. There were men and women working in those gardens, stopping momentarily to wave their hands at the passengers looking out the train windows.

Slowly the daily train eased into the area where a platform and small wooden station with a tiny waiting room had been built. Snowhook could see Harry Boyles standing on the platform as he descended the stairs of the train coach. Around him were other passengers who indicated their excitement about visiting Penney Farms for the first time.

The farmer shook the reporter's hand explaining that his wife was at a mission society meeting of the Penney women and the boys were in school.

"You mean you have a church here already?" asked the surprised visitor.

"Well, yes, these wives all come from churches back home and there was already a church here called the Community Church just down the road by the big dairy barn. Mr. Clark also turned one of the bigger houses over to us as a meeting place. It's just down the street from here."

The reporter looked with interest in all directions as the two men began their visit of Penney Farms. They walked past the large canning factory with its huge water tower and Snowhook saw clouds of dust raised by plows being pulled by mules led by hardworking black men.

"What's the large stone building over there?" the reporter asked as he pointed easterly beyond the gardens being plowed. "I noticed it as we pulled into here. It looks like an army fortress."

Harry laughed, "Yeh, in a way, it's going to be a fortress, our spiritual fortress. It's the Penney Memorial Church that Mr. Penney is building in memory of his parents."

"I hadn't been aware of something else alongside of the farm experiment."

"Oh, it's more than the church. A number of cottages are

also being built around the church and it's going to be a retirement community for retired ministers, missionaries and YMCA workers."

Shrugging his shoulders as they kept walking down the dirt road toward the center of town, the Baltimore reporter began jotting on a pad he'd pulled out of his suitcoat pocket. Then he said, "I understand you have three plantings a year here."

"Yes, and those men behind the mules plowing, along with the agricultural experts brought in by Mr. Penney, are hoping to really make this the farm showplace of America."

"How can they do anything with the kind of sandy soil you have here?" the visitor asked as they began to walk by the school which Jeremiah and Samuel attended.

"They're convinced they can change that soil. So, we have a lab in that building opposite the school where they do analysis, demonstration planting, and in that garage over there they have the latest up-to-date equipment available."

"Very impressive," said Snowhook, as he stopped to write more notes.

Harry added, "And those of us who came here are taking courses on agronomy at the Institute, we're a very interesting mix of nationalities and religions."

"What do you mean by 'an interesting mix?'" the reporter asked as he kept scribbling.

"Well, for example, over there to the west of us we have a farm run by Mr. Travassos, a Portuguese farmer from Boston, who came here with his family and is doing very well.

"Down that other road we have a Mr. Gunther, who is of

German background from the Philadelphia area, and over there close to our farm is a neighbor who's from Ohio.

"We all came knowing the risk we would run and believing this is one of the most important experiments of the twentieth century."

"And you believe it's working?" the reporter asked somewhat skeptically.

"Over 20,000 acres have been cleared. They're building 50 more farmhouses in addition to these that you see all along Penney Road. Which, by the way, Mr. Penney put in with the pavement.

"We also have a staff visiting all over the country to interview people who have heard of us. They're told about the team who will help them, the twenty acres of land and house they're provided, rent-free for the first year, and of course they must have between $750 and $1,000 to help them get through that time. When they get their first crop they keep every penny they've earned."

At this point in their walking, Snowhook saw southward a pasture filled with hundreds of cows. He pointed toward them, "And how many of those do you have?"

"We have over 3,000 head, plus pigs, sheep, hens and goats, and are doing a lot with animals as well as garden products."

Suddenly a Model T Ford passed them and two men waved at the walkers.

"That's Pop Ramey," said Harry as he waved back. "He has Clark Failing with him. They've just come back from Starke where they buy dynamite to blow up the stumps that the sawmills left there when they moved out of here after they went bankrupt. Those men direct the digging of wells and the draining of swampy soil. In fact they're helping do that over in the area where they're building the new cottages for the retirement community."

"I'm amazed," said the reporter, as Harry Boyles led him to see the office of the Farm Center, the hotel where guests stayed, the swimming pool that had been put in for the residents, the house built for a doctor, the building erected for agricultural classrooms, the gasoline station which was having more business as cars became more popular, and the agricultural working library. He saw acres of grapevines, potatoes, tomatoes, and even peppermint which Harry Boyles said was supplying the Beechnut gum people and shipped all over the world.

At the general store, Snowhook bought postcards to take back to Maryland and some licorice candy to send back to the Boyles children. Then he took a bus back to Green Cove Springs urging Boyles as he left to explain to the boys that he didn't have time to see their calf or their hens but he would be back.

John Snowhook returned to Baltimore convinced that the Penney-Gwinn Corporation had indeed created a model for putting new life into the rural economy of the United States. In fact, he was also hearing of the visits of people from Europe and Asia. He reported that self-sufficiency was the mark of J.C. Penney which was about to change the direction of farming everywhere in the world.

However, several things began to work against the agricultural project. In spite of the brilliance of men like Dr. D.W. Morton, former dean of the School of Commerce and Business Administration at the University of California; Burdette Lewis, former commissioner in New York, who became the president of Foremost Dairies in Penney Farms; Francis Clark, dean of Berea College who became the supervisor and farm manager; and other colleagues with tremendous credentials, the Penney Farms yielded smaller crops than expected and low prices in a declining economy began to affect their marketing.

Many of the farmers became discouraged and began working at other jobs to keep going. In the next few years, when they had hoped to have 6,000 farms established in the area, there were less than 100 in operation.

With all the hopes of improving the sandy soil, the reality was that the clay sub-soil was impossible to change. The garden-growing just didn't materialize. That, plus the extreme heat, the struggle against bugs and animals, and the health problems encountered by families served to drive people away from the farm dream.

Mr. Penney was dismayed to find the morale of staff and farmers at a low level. He put his son Roswell in charge for one year and then, on the brink of disaster, announced that the Agricultural Institute would be closed and the remaining farmers were on their own.

In 1932, after trying to negotiate with creditors hoping to find some group willing to take over the Farms Project, J.C. Penney met with Paul Rheinhold, a successful Pittsburgh dairyman, who agreed to restructure the Penney Foremost

Dairy Corporation into Foremost Properties Inc., of Jacksonville. With Mr. Rheinhold serving as its president the Florida holdings of the Penney-Gwinn Corporation were transferred to Foremost Properties and the rural-magic dream of J.C. Penney ended.

About the time that the farm endeavor was nearing its termination, Mr. Penney said in an address he gave, "Any experimental scheme is always filled with risks. It has been my observation through the years that when a need arises good always lays a burden upon somebody's shoulders. The human race has discovered and been blessed with a glorious host of persons who found their chief joy in bearing the burdens of others."

After the failure of the Penney Farms endeavor there are no records of his expressing regrets over the tremendous effort and expense that he put forward on behalf of farmers. If anything, he began to speak more frequently about his own spiritual development which came through the times of hardship and struggle. Undiscouraged, he still had a bigger plan for Penney Farms.

CHAPTER VIII

VILLAGE ON THE RIVER

IT WAS A DRIPPING, HOT DAY ON SEPTEMBER 19, 1925, WHEN A perspiring load of passengers bounced their way into Green Cove Springs on the old rattling bus out of Jacksonville.

As the noisy vehicle approached the St. Elmo Hotel, just one block up from the St. Johns River, the riders peered out expectantly through the dirty, steamy windows.

The Rev. and Mrs. R.A. Cody, with their son, Joseph, were sitting in the overcrowded bus as the driver announced they were about to arrive at their destination.

The family from Tennessee looked curiously at the people standing outside the hotel waiting for the bus. Mrs. Cody leaned over and whispered to her husband, "I hope we haven't made a mistake in coming here." Her son, upon hearing his mother's anxious words, reached over and gripped her hand as if to say, "Everything will be fine, Mom," but in his heart he wasn't too sure. Her husband didn't respond as he looked away from her trying to catch a glimpse of the one who might be waiting for them.

The bus squeaked to a stop and the driver advised the passengers to retrieve their suitcases and packages from the overhead racks. The door opened and they each inched their way out of the bus and stepped onto the ground of the place they'd heard so much about.

A voice hailed the three as they struggled with their suitcases and packages. "Hello there!" someone yelled, while waving his arms. "Are you the Codys from Tennessee?"

They saw a distinguished well-dressed man emerge from behind other waiting people.

With a positive response from the father, the stranger reached for a large suitcase that Mrs. Cody was trying to manage. "I'm Walter Morton," he explained as she released the bag and gave a smile of relief. "I'm the manager of the new Penney Retirement Community which we're opening up here at Green Cove Springs. I could tell from the picture you sent me of your family that you are indeed the ones I've been waiting for, and this must be Joseph." With this he reached out and patted the boy on the back. "Nice to have you here finally," he said.

"What a relief to have you meet us," explained Mr. Cody, "we've been on the road many days and are about at our wit's end." Mrs. Cody heaved a heavy sigh of relief indicating her pleasure in meeting this man. "We weren't sure who was going to meet us, Dr. Morton," she said, "but you sure look good to us, in the middle of this strange town."

After shaking hands and guiding the newcomers through the gathered crowd, Walter Morton led them into the lobby of the hotel. Young Joseph looked about at the Queen Victoria-type furniture and the brightly colored rugs and asked, "Is this it? Is this where we're going to live?"

"Oh, no," responded Morton, sensing that the boy was a little confused and not yet knowing that Joseph had left Lebanon, Tennessee, with great reluctance and even signs of rebellion. "This hotel was built to take care of the overflow of people who wanted to stay at the Qui-Si-Sana Hotel just a few blocks from here."

"That's a funny name," laughed Joseph.

"It means 'Here is Health' and it's named that because it has the warm springs right next to it." Then he added, as he led the family to the registration desk, "Mr. Penney owns that other hotel and he even has an office there."

"Will we see that?" the boy asked excitedly as his father spoke to the hotel clerk and began signing in.

"After you register here and we get your suitcases into your room, I will take you down to the pool so you can see the main attraction in this town."

As Mrs. Cody took her son's hand and whispered to him, telling him he was monopolizing the conversation too much, she smiled at Dr. Morton and said, "The boy has been pretty anxious about coming to this place with us. It's so far away from home and his friends and so different. He begged us to allow him to stay with his grandmother."

Morton nodded understandingly and the three Codys walked to their room on the first floor while their host took a seat in the lobby. As he watched the family disappear down the corridor he noticed for the first time that they were dressed in heavy fall clothing. Joseph had on wool knickers, a shirt and sweater, and even wore a wool cap. The parents were also dressed in clothing foreign to the Florida climate. A few minutes later, the family returned to the lobby and Morton said, "I'm sure you've discovered it's pretty warm here at this time of year. In fact it's 90 degrees on the outside hotel thermometer."

"We noticed how hot it was and suffered on that crowded bus. We know we're overdressed but didn't want to hold you up," responded Mrs. Cody.

"Why don't you change into some different clothing so you can be more comfortable," Dr. Morton asked thoughtfully. "I'm in no hurry."

The family agreed they should go back to their room and change. They quickly returned to Morton expressing appreciation of his thoughtfulness and the joy of the Florida warmth.

"What we'll do now," said Morton, "is hop aboard my Lizzie and take a look at the area, starting with the spring and pool and then we'll head up the river to the place where you'll live."

"When do you think that will happen?" Mrs. Cody asked as the three slipped onto the seats of his car.

"Perhaps a few more days. We've had some men working on the cottages. They're just a little north of here. And you can stay here at the St. Elmo until your place is ready for occupancy. Mr. Penney will pay all your hotel bills and meals during that time."

"That's certainly generous of him," responded Robert Cody. "Are there others here yet?"

"No," answered Walter Morton, as he started up the car and headed toward the spring and pool. "In fact, you are the first family to arrive." This was a surprise to the Cody family.

They arrived at the Qui-Si-Sana Hotel and saw many people at the lovely Spanish-designed hotel, with the crowded swimming pool next to it.

Morton explained that the pool had a year 'round temperature of 78 degrees and was fed by an artesian well which pumped 3,000 gallons of sulphur water into it every hour from fifty feet below.

"The water is constantly replenished and an overflow system channels it into the river so it's always fresh, pure and healthy. That's why so many people have come from a distance to enjoy its benefits."

The pool was glass-enclosed and divided into a section for men, women, and children, with a special section "for coloreds only." Joseph whispered to his parents, "I sure didn't expect to see that here."

"Well," his dad reminded him, "we are still in the South, and it's going to take a long time to change the thinking here."

From the popular spring and pool, Dr. Morton drove the family northward on the river road. There were beautiful southern mansions, some with white columns on the front, and newer smaller houses, recently built in the late 1900s and early twenties which were more indicative of the changes taking place in that community. They were excited to catch glimpses of the river with its glassy surface of blue, green and purple mixtures. Dr. Morton stopped the car by one of the docks at the end of a connecting path, while the four of them silently watched sailboats gliding by with the occasional appearances of tugboats towing barges to Jacksonville or Palatka.

As they progressed northward Walter Morton said, "We're now on the way to the old sawmill, which was formerly owned by the Dowling-Shands Lumber Company. That burned down a few years ago and Mr. Penney bought the land there as part of the 120,000 acres he purchased through the new corporation that he formed with his attorney Mr. Gwinn. The corporation bought it at a court auction."

"Is that where we're going to live?" queried Mrs. Cody as though trying to visualize what it would be like to live next to a burned down sawmill.

"Yes," responded Morton as he turned off the river road to the main road leading to Fleming Island and, further on, Jacksonville. "But all that's left is the foundation on one side of the road and over thirty cottages on the other side."

As the car approached the old lumber camp and sawmill, they began to see the cluster of cottages not far from the road. Just beyond was a wooden bridge crossing Governor's Creek, and to the right a dock with boats tied up to it on the river's edge.

The family's eyes were flashing with excitement as they each took in the breathtaking panorama where they would soon be living. They were overwhelmed by the cypress trees and live oaks with huge trunks and crooked branches reaching out while seeming to wave the delicate bunches of Spanish moss in the river's breeze.

"The bridge," explained Morton, "crosses Governor's Creek and, Joseph, it's a great place to fish, as is the dock on the river."

As he turned his car onto a rutted road on the left, they saw it high with weeds and surrounded by the cottages, some in greater disrepair than others. Suddenly some squirrels ran in front of the car as the guide jammed his brakes on.

"How about that," Mr. Cody exclaimed, "even the squirrels have come out to welcome us, the Pilgrims from Tennessee."

"But they're smaller and skinnier than what we had back home," offered his wife.

"What's that?" Joseph shouted excitedly as they began to get out of the car. It was an animal crawling by which he'd never seen before. He watched fascinated as it disappeared into the bushes toward the river.

"Oh, that's a baby alligator," explained Walter Morton. "They're harmless...in fact it was probably born not long ago."

The sun was just beginning to set in the west putting on a show of splashed paintbrush-pink spread over the cottony clouds.

They walked among the cottages seeing signs of the workmanship of the carpenters. New boards were piled up, bags of cement were stacked, and kegs of nails dotted the area. They could even smell the new sawdust that was left by some tables erected by the workers.

"Looks like they've been working. So, let's head back before dark and have some supper at the hotel. Tomorrow we'll come back here and take a closer look," said Morton as the family climbed into the car, regretting that the shadows were coming all too soon for them to see more.

After a hot restless night, the Cody family met the manager for breakfast in the hotel cafe. Then they headed for Governor's Creek and the future site of their new home.

On the way Morton retold the story about J.C. Penney's establishment of the new farms and the Institute for Agricultural Studies at Long Branch which was just eight miles west of them.

Upon arriving at the sawmill location the manager of the new project parked the car, turned off the engine and said, "You are now looking at the result of a dream Mr. Penney had just a few months ago."

Mrs. Cody thought, *You call this a dream? It looks like a nightmare to me.*

Almost as though answering the wife and mother, Dr. Morton went on, "Some people will wonder about Mr. Penney's sanity, but when you talk with him about his dreams you come away convinced that it was as real as Jacob's dream at Haran. You feel that God was truly in the prayers and thoughts of this great man."

The Rev. R.A. Cody felt as though he was hearing a sermon from a spokesman of God. He also felt the negative vibes from his wife as she looked at the sawmill ruins, the partially destroyed cottages and the isolated jungle around them. The palmetto bushes and thickets seemed to signal the potential for being swallowed up by nature.

Joseph saw a different picture as he pointed with

enthusiasm to birds he'd never seen before. Dr. Morton identified snowy egrets, mocking birds, and a group of ibis. He
also indicated an eagle's nest close to them as Rev. Mr. Cody
called attention to an eagle in the nest peeking over the side
as though wary of their invasion.

Walter Morton added to his previous thoughts by saying,
"I'm sure what you see here may shake you up a bit but,
remember, it's just the beginning of what Mr. Penney believes
is God's plan for special people like you...something like the
way God gave a special land to His people."

Mrs. Cody said, hesitatingly, "I have to be honest with
you, Dr. Morton, I expected something different...or at least
ready for us."

"Remember," Morton said as he hastened to reassure the
woman, "we've got men working on this project. They're a
little behind schedule because of some jobs they've had to do
at the Long Branch farms, but you can stay at the St. Elmo
Hotel 'til your place is ready."

"I can see the great possibilities here," injected Robert
Cody hoping to cheer up his wife.

Just then a truck drove up with a number of workmen in
the back. They hopped out with saws, axes, hammers, and
other tools in their hands.

Dr. Morton talked with the foreman of the job while the
Codys began to look more closely at the grounds and the cottages. They learned later that the manager was urging the
workers to give quick attention to the cottage nearest
Governor's Creek so that the new family could move in without much delay.

Returning to the Codys he led them down a path to the dock on the river. On the way he said, "It's amazing how Mr. Penney has been led by God to think of a special community here for ministers and YMCA workers with their families, who even might have financial or health needs. He honestly believes there can be a Christian community here which will be something like the place where the early Christians lived together, just as we read about it in the Book of Acts."

"How did he happen to come to this dream? After all, he had started the farm project for farmers and that was quite a lot," the minister said.

"You're asking the right question, and some of Mr. Penney's financial advisors have warned him about extending himself. But we must remember his father was a minister and a farmer. He prayed a lot about it and one night, after he had visited Moose Haven Retirement Home, founded a few years ago for members of the Moose Lodge, he began thinking seriously about doing something for ministers and YMCA workers who were sacrificing their lives on behalf of others.

"That night he awoke with this struggle tearing his soul apart. He began to pray and heard God say to him, *James Penney, remember your past and your parents. Remember how they faithfully followed the Lord Jesus Christ, pouring out their lives for the Holy cause. Yet they never had the opportunity 'as saints from their labor resting'...never had the experience of quiet enjoyment or empowering renewal. Using this land I have given you as a memorial to your parents will bring rest, health, and happiness to many such saints!*"

84

"That's a tremendous decision," exclaimed Cody, "and a great risk."

"J.C. Penney was never afraid of risk, if he felt it was because God willed it."

As they stood on the dock touched by the beauty around them, Mrs. Cody responded to the scene enveloping them and the words of Dr. Morton.

"I feel like singing, "Shall We Gather at the River," for that hymn suddenly takes on new meaning for me."

The foreman of the workers caught up with them and said, "Sir, that cottage nearest Governor's Creek is in better shape than we had thought. Perhaps it can be lived in sooner than we expected. That is, if the family is willing to put up with a few inconveniences."

"Like what?" queried the manager, as they began to walk back toward the cottage.

"Well, we still don't have running water but there's a working well just 100 feet from that cottage, the inside plumbing isn't in yet but if they're willing to use the out-house over in the back, and willing to be without screens they can move in right away."

"What about furniture?" asked Mrs. Cody with eagerness in her voice.

"We don't have any in yet, but we have spare beds, chairs, cots, and wardrobes stored at the Qui-Si-Sana, which you can use if you're willing to be pioneers."

The Codys looked at each other and at the unfinished cottage. Each gave a signal to the other indicating their willingness to demonstrate their trust in Dr. Morton and his workers.

With adrenaline flowing the new family began to see the full picture. They were the first members of the new retirement community. They felt the responsibility of affirming Mr. Penney's actions inspired by his prayer life.

Robert Cody put his arms around his wife and boy and suggested they have a word of prayer. The nearby workers removed their caps and put down their tools, while Walter Morton nodded approvingly.

"O God," the minister prayed, "as we stand on this sacred spot as the first residents of this new community, we come overwhelmed by your goodness.

"We feel the way your servant Abraham felt when You told him to leave his homestead and move to a new place. We've done this, Lord, believing, risking, and supported by the leadership of Mr. Penney and the workers who surround him.

"We hear your voice speaking to us with the same words You spoke to Abraham, when You said, 'Do not be afraid, I am your shield.'

"We know You are with us, guiding and helping us.

"We praise You as we place our lives in your hands.

"Walk with us as we confess our unworthiness and our needs.

"In Jesus' Name. Amen."

There was a time of holy quietness as the workers tiptoed back to their work and Walter Morton led the family back to the car without a word spoken by anyone.

The next day the family returned to the cottage next to Governor's Creek. The workers had already moved in the basic furnishings before they arrived.

They were beginning to live the first days of the long journey planned for this new and different village on the river.

CHAPTER IX

PENMOR PLACE

THIRTEEN DAYS AFTER THE ARRIVAL OF THE CODYS TO GREEN COVE Springs, Florida, the Rev. G.F. Kinnear, his wife, Evelyn, and his son, Riley, arrived in the pouring rain at the old saw mill site where a restored cottage was waiting for them.

"How wonderful to find you here," said George Kinnear as he struggled to find a place to set his suitcases because of the mud and puddles. "We were told back in Canton, Ohio, that we would be here alone."

"No," responded Robert Cody as he extended one hand to shake and helped lift some small bags with the other. "We've been here as the so-called 'lonely ones' but not really between Dr. and Mrs. Morton's visits, the wonderful daytime presence of the workmen and the curiosity visits of these squirrels."

"And don't forget the visits of the alligator," added Joseph, "that crawls up from Governor's Creek to see what's happening here."

"Oh!" gasped Evelyn Kinnear, "I hope we're not in any danger!"

Trying to turn the conversation to a subject less threatening to his wife, Mr. Kinnear said, "All I've read in preparation for coming here is that gators won't bother us if we don't bother them. But, I want to say how reassuring it is to find you folks here and especially to see your son talking with Riley over there. His fear was that he would find himself as the only boy among a lot of preachers."

"The purpose of this new village is to help retired ministers, missionaries and YMCA workers," responded Cody, "but as they explained to us in Lebanon, Tennessee, which is where we come from, when we had our first interview with a Penney official, Mr. Penney felt it would take time to get the word out to potential retirees. So, with things as they are, especially for ministers like us, the first years here will be open to clergy and Y workers who may have health problems or financial difficulties."

"We happen to be in both categories," said Mrs. Kinnear as Mrs. Cody approached them from her cottage. "This invitation has been a godsend because George has been without a church for over a year and I've had chronic bronchitis for a long time."

At this point in the getting-acquainted conversation, the young Kinnear boy approached his parents with Joseph at his side and expressed a desire to go with Joseph down to the creek. He was far more interested in seeing if he could see an alligator or some other new creature than he was in seeing their new home in the cottage. With permission granted, the parents followed the Codys to their new living place, bent upon settling their cottage while the rain had stopped momentarily.

Within a week the Rev. and Mrs. J.R. Skinner of Winamac, Indiana, arrived followed by the George Halls and their sons, Kenneth, Merrill, Donald and Clarence, who came from Mt. Ayres, Iowa. Then others arrived, almost daily, filling the cottages which were not yet fully prepared for comfortable living. However, the men soon discovered, as they got better acquainted and tools were borrowed from the farm project at Long Branch, that they each had skills not usually associated with clergy or YMCA workers. They were then able to pitch in and step up the pace of cottage repairs.

Several other ministers arrived with their spouses and sons which led Riley Kinnear to raise the question as to why no girls were being welcomed to the new community.

In November, two "girls" did arrive, but they were in their sixties. Each was a widow of a former missionary. Mrs. Mary I. Begen of Illinois had served with her husband for thirty-two years as a Presbyterian missionary in China. The other was Mrs. Mattie Wright of Wooster, Ohio, who had served with her husband as a missionary to Persia.

An exciting day did arrive for the boys at the new community when the Rev. and Mrs. A.J. Noblett of Tyler, Texas, arrived with son Roy and daughter Virginia, who was a pretty young teenager.

Families continued to arrive filling up all the cottages which the combined efforts of the Penney carpenters and the skilled residents had made ready.

With a fast declining economy in the nation and the assurance by Mr. Penney that none of these new residents would have to pay anything for their housing and care, the response of potential newcomers increased. Soon more YMCA laypeople were arriving, led by Mr. W.A. Wilson and his wife, a retired Y staff-person from Maplewood, New Jersey. Around this time a professor named Dr. Ferguson moved into a restored cottage but being older and sicker than all the others he had to be moved to a hospital in Jacksonville where he soon passed away.

All together, by the end of January, 1926, there were sixty-four residents living in the still uncompleted cottages. Through the months the people there saw a growing unity and an amazingly harmonious spirit. With each visit that J.C. Penney made among them he commented on the good feelings he got and the fulfillment he felt in having this new community develop. He also had Dr. Morton and his workers enlarge one of the cottages to make it into a meeting place for the residents.

As the group grew in number, several of the preachers drew upon their organizational backgrounds and at one meeting proposed the establishment of a Residents Association. Its purpose was to be "for the interest and welfare of all." On November 25, 1925, the association was brought into being and the Rev. George Metzel was elected as its first president. Mr. Cody was named chairman of the Welcoming Committee.

Meeting in the new community building, the Rev. Edward Layport suggested that they come up with a name for the new community. After much discussion it became apparent that half the group wanted it to be named "The Penney Community" and the other half wanted it to be named "The Morton Community."

The Rev. George Hall got to his feet and said, "Mr. Penney made this place possible and should be honored by our using his name. On the other hand, Dr. Morton has given of himself, his talents and dedication to help us get off to a good start. They both should be honored and I'd like to suggest that we combine their names and call it Pen- (for Penney) mor (for Morton)."

The residents liked the idea of compromise and eventually decided to call it Penmor Place.

Thereafter new events took place at Penmor Place, such as their first Thanksgiving when the men went down to the river dock and using bamboo poles they stood on the rickety structure and pulled in a large number of fish. The women prepared vegetables brought to them from the Long Branch farms. Desserts were numerous as they reflected the various backgrounds of the residents.

As they sat around the tables at the Community Hall it was obvious that they were a thankful people even though their "turkey" was fried fish and their weather was in the nineties. After the meal they went to worship—some to St. Margaret's Episcopal on Fleming Island (the oldest Episcopal church in Clay County), some to the Baptist church, and others to the Presbyterian and Methodist churches. Their scattering to different churches reflected the ecumenical pattern which was emerging in their history-making growth.

During the Thanksgiving dinner, Dr. and Mrs. Morton arrived and brought some homemade ice cream to the delight of all. While eating with the families Mrs. Morton whispered that she heard Mr. Penney tell her husband he planned to provide the Christmas dinner that was only a month away.

George Metzel, Resident Association President, liked the idea and named a committee to make plans for the Christmas celebration.

On Christmas day they gathered again in a festively-decorated hall and the tables were loaded with turkeys, stuffing, creamed potatoes, string beans and squash, cranberry sauce and plum puddings. A tree had been erected in one corner of the hall and a disguised Santa Claus gave out presents to each of the seventy in attendance.

Other social gatherings took place, such as a Valentine party where Mr. Penney and Ralph Gwinn took part. Each of these occasions were marked by much wit and humor. The community was learning to laugh together.

On March 13, 1926, the first 50th anniversary of a marriage occurred when Dr. and Mrs. J.R. Skinner were honored at Penmor Place for their many years of marriage. At this party there was a humorous mock wedding with the original bride and groom taking part. It turned out to be what the residents called "a jolly time."

Regularly scheduled events were part of their life. Prayer meetings were held each Wednesday night in the community hall. Small groups of men gathered in one or two empty cottages for woodworking which resulted in new chairs, tables, bookcases, cupboards and desks. The women had sewing, knitting, and rug-making groups.

The whole community of Green Cove Springs was aware of the many activities and the good spirit which were manifested at Penmor Place.

On the night of March 16, 1925, the residents of Penmor Place arrived at the Community Hall for their regular midweek prayer service. They were bundled up in heavy coats, several layers of clothing, knit stocking caps, and mittens and gloves. It was unusually cold outside. But a small woodstove took off the chill as people entered and found their seats.

"There'll be a good crowd tonight, what with Mr. Penney coming and Dr. Poling giving the Bible study," one said.

Another added, "I never expected to see thirty-five degrees down here, but the fellowship will warm things up."

And sure enough as they entered the hall, got their hymnbooks and tried to sit near the woodstove there was a warmth, not only from the stove, but from the expectancy of seeing Mr. Penney and Dr. Daniel Poling.

Hymns were sung enthusiastically while Mrs. Kinnear played on a little pump organ. Prayers were offered spontaneously. Then the presider introduced Dr. Poling and suggested that the Philadelphia pastor share some biblical thoughts which would strengthen them as a Christian community.

The famous pastor shared his thoughts based upon Roman 12. He said, "Romans 12:4-8 has several verses which I want to underscore as the basis of growth for each of you here at Penmor Place.

"The Apostle Paul is writing to a relatively new church in Rome and he's reminding them about their being joined together as one body, each with different parts and each with different functions.

"He also reminded them that their different gifts might be as teachers, as preachers, as leaders and as followers, but basic to the unity sought is the willingness to share. This," he added, "is offering oneself as volunteers in service. And the process is described in verse 8—where Paul writes, 'Whoever shares with others should do it generously, whoever has authority should work hard, whoever shows kindness to others should do it cheerfully.'"

After some further elaboration on the subject, "The Secret of Unity," which is sharing gifts as cheerful volunteers, Dr. Poling suggested that this theme could become the motto of the new community. Then he added, "Now that I've laid a scriptural foundation for each of you, I want to share an announcement that Mr. Penney should be making but he asked me to do it on his behalf." There was a strange quietness in that hall. *What now?* they thought.

Dr. Poling continued, "As Mr. Penney came to know you this winter while attending meetings in your homes, or here at this community hall, he is gratified with what he's seen and heard. Because of this he has decided to make your homes more substantial and permanent."

He paused as people gasped, looked at each other, and whispered thoughts trying to guess what this all meant.

Sensing the response of the residents, Dr. Poling continued, "Mr. Penney has decided that these cottages are not good enough for you and so he plans to erect a new one hundred-apartment building as a memorial to his father and mother."

When he finished speaking there was a stunned people sitting in shock as they dabbed at their eyes while still trying to absorb the significance of the announcement.

On the way back to their cottages the surprised people chatted excitedly about the good news. One of them shared what George Metzel told him on the way out, that Mr. Penney had said that he was going to build a three-story building right at the old sawmill site. Which is why he had built a paved road with curbs in the Governor's Creek area of the town.

The next day the Clay County newspaper had a lead article about the projected apartment house for the Penmor Place community. From that time on it was all downhill for the Penney construction plan. The local residents met with the Town Council and protested the "rich man's invasion" of their town. One of them said at the council meeting, "That rich Yankee has put in a new road at the north end of Green Cove Springs with curbstones and trees. The other residents of the town are so curious about that end of town they're all driving there with their families. With all that traffic they're endangering the lives of those of us who have lived peacefully in that area for years."

A high-level meeting was held with Mr. Penney, Dr. Walter Morton, Francis Clark and Ralph Gwinn to discuss the mounting opposition of the townspeople to the newly projected plan.

Francis Clark made an impassioned plea for a change in plans. He suggested that 50 or 60 acres of the land owned by the Penney-Gwinn Corporation at Long Branch could be deeded over to a new corporation which would provide space for a retirement community.

Dr. Morton suggested that Penmor Place be closed out or moved to the location just eight miles west of their present location. Ralph Gwinn proposed that the new retirement community could be called "Memorial Home Community" as a tribute to the parents of Mr. Penney. The group enthusiastically supported the change and Mr. Penney proposed that he would have papers drawn up, and an architect secured to build a church with cottages around it. He would pay for all this to take place. It would be a fitting tribute to his father and mother.

CHAPTER X

THE INVITATION

IT WAS WEDNESDAY NIGHT PRAYER MEETING TIME AT THE Bordenville Community Church. People came down the road on a spring-like April evening. They came in cars, on horseback, and walking.

Manuel and María Travassos came up the mule team road with their eight children. It was only a fifteen-minute walk from their farm at Long Branch (later called Penney Farms.)

As they approached the little one-room wooden church they saw the Rev. Mr. Conway, their pastor and warm friend. He spotted them and called out, "Good evening, Brother Manuel, glad you and Sister María could come out tonight, and especially to see you have all the children with you."

"Nice to see you," responded Manuel Travassos, as he hastened to help tie up the palomino which the pastor rode up to the railing at the front of the church. "We had to get a neighbor to milk our cows because I wanted us all here, especially tonight."

The lanky rugged-looking pastor dismounted and reached out, shaking the hands of the entire Travassos family. This was one of his most faithful families and Manuel was one of his most dependable deacons. Tonight was going to be more than the usual singing, praying, testifying get-together.

As the Travassos entered, greeting other members who had arrived, they took up an entire pew, Nathan, Ruth, Rachel, Asenath, Elizabeth, Abraham, Esther and little Job. Manuel and María had done a good job in raising their children since their arrival from Boston at the invitation of Mr. Penney.

They had settled on their twenty-acre farm near Kentucky Avenue in response to the offer of the Penney-Gwinn Agricultural experiment that brought more than one hundred families to establish a farm on the acreage that J.C. Penney and his staff of experts were developing.

The little Bordenville Community Church, just down the road a way, toward Middlebury, had grown under the leadership of Pastor Conway who was a good preacher and a good pastor. Many of the new farmers and their families had come to the church to fellowship with others including those at the Institute for Applied Agriculture.

As the pastor led them in a hymn and prayer, María Travassos felt strange sensations of anxiety, for their minister looked worn and burdened. She wondered what was bothering him? Then he spoke,

"Ever since the laying of the cornerstone of the new Memorial Home Chapel last June, we have all watched with great interest as changes began to take place on that sixty acres of land that Mr. Penney has designated as a memorial to his parents.

"We've seen a beautiful, cathedral-like building rise up in the center of the community, surrounded by buildings containing apartments for retired religious workers and their spouses."

As he talked, Manuel's memory mechanism began to function. He saw and heard the buzzing chain saws as they tumbled the scrub oaks, pine trees, and palmetto bushes. He recalled walking with the children to the acreage being cleared, noting how swampy it was, overrun with raccoons, skunks, rabbits, snakes, and even alligators. He saw the men blasting stumps and running pumps to drain the area. He remembered standing by the train tracks and watching load after load of dirt being dumped or carried by the mule-wagons to places needing fill.

He marveled at the rapidity of the elevation of the tower and roof of the new church. He heard about the carloads of cement that were dumped for the foundation of the tower. Some people said that it looked like a cathedral erected in a French town.

Once in a while he would peek inside the church, when the workers had all disappeared for the day, and stand in awe under the sweeping arches which were hewn by hand from surrounding cedars and native cypress trees cut at the Penney-Gwinn property just west of Long Branch.

He remembered hearing Mr. Penney speak and saying, "I want this chapel to rise above the homes which will surround it as a reminder of the centrality of the Lord Jesus Christ and the constant presence of God the Father."

He was awakened from his recall dreaming as his pastor's melodious voice pronounced the "amen" to his long prayer. Then Rev. Mr. Conway said, "Today is a crucial day in the life of the Bordenville Community Church because of what we see happening a short distance from here.

"I've invited Bascom Franklin to be with us because we all know him. He has worshiped with us many times, and we have seen his wonderful leadership at the Agricultural Center since coming here from Berea College in Kentucky. We have watched him give guidance as the supervisor of maintenance and the director of construction of the Memorial Chapel and the cottages which surround it."

Mr. Franklin came forward from the back of the church and stood at eye level in front of the people in the pews. Speaking in a slow, halting fashion, he said, "I appreciate your pastor's invitation to talk briefly with you this evening, because I'm well aware of some anxiety and possible confusion which is bound to exist in a church when a new church is being built just up the road."

With this he paused, as he noticed some of the members nodding to each other and recalled momentarily how word had come to him of some farmers referring to the new community being built as "The Holy City" and the other day he heard one of them, at the village store, make a sneering comment about "The Houses of Lords."

He went on, "Ever since the laying of the church cornerstone on June 13, 1926, we have all seen the clearing of the land, the building of the church Mr. Penney calls the Chapel, the arrival of students and faculty from Berea College to help their former professor with the construction of the twenty-two apartments, some of which are already occupied by the new residents.

"I don't know how many of you have seen those apartments, but at the dedication coming up you will be able to visit them. Each has three rooms and a bath, totally furnished with kitchens having refrigerators, electric and oil stoves, cupboard space, with a central fireplace in the living room.

"This coming Sunday the 24th of April, 1927, we will climax three days of celebration and dedication as we complete the year's efforts to realize the fulfillment of Mr. Penney's dream to honor the memory of his mother and father.

"Yesterday, we mounted a tablet in the vestibule of the church which reads as follows: 'In the thirteenth century in France, particularly in Normandy, the houses and dwellings of the inhabitants were built near the churches which often were built by the laymen and the clergy themselves with their own hands...simplicity predominated, lines and forms in good proportion and as in good scale served to give a charm without...any elaborate decoration...it is because of these precedents that we have established the style of architecture which you see here.'"

One of the farmers leaned over to whisper to his wife, "Who's he trying to kid? It all looks pretty uppity to me. I understand they're even going to build a golf course there."

Mr. Franklin sensed there were some hostile feelings in the group he was addressing so he turned to Rev. Mr. Conway and asked, "May I share what you and I were discussing before this meeting began?"

"By all means," the minister responded. "You have my permission."

"Well," continued Bascom Franklin, "word has come to us that some of the members of the Bordenville Community Church are upset. It's been reported that Mr. Penney's intention is to put the Bordenville Community Church out of business the way his big Penney stores put little merchants out of business. This is not so. Mr. Penney wants to offer the use of the new chapel building as a place where we can do something cooperatively to the glory of God.

"We could become a true community church, nondenominational, utilizing the educational facility we offer, and worshiping with the uplift of our new pipe organ given as a memorial to Mr. Gwinn's mother. We could become a unified witness in this community."

He paused briefly to let the significance of the offer he was making sink in and then he continued, "In addition we would like to invite your pastor, the Rev. Mr. Conway, to become the pastor of the new Chapel in the Memorial Home Community, preaching every other Sunday with the other ministers sharing the pulpit on the alternate Sundays."

One of the women raised her hand to ask a question. "Is our pastor open to this idea? I'd like to hear from him."

Mr. Conway stood up and replied, "I have no problems with such an arrangement because we are both community churches, close to each other, and facing tremendous possibilities for growth, larger Christian education facilities, and offering a new, fresh approach to this community. But let us attend the dedication services next weekend and take some time for prayer and discussion. Then we will decide as a church what we think God's will is for each of us."

The members nodded in approval of his suggestion and after the benediction many of them gathered around Mr. Franklin with questions to be asked.

Upon arriving back at the farmhouse the Travassos family sat around the wood stove while María Travassos served them cups of hot chocolate. Ruth, their oldest daughter, noticed that as they walked the dark path back, with the moon peeking through the trees, no one said anything about the meeting and the invitation from Mr. Franklin. Their quietness seemed to signal deep thoughts about the church meeting. She looked over at her father who, with his bearded face and chiseled features, always made her think of Moses in the Old Testament days. He had a look of noble character and a way of manifesting wisdom that influenced her.

"Pa," she said breaking into the silence of the family, "why is Mr. Penney doing all this? Like building a new church when we already have one here, or bringing in all those preachers and their families, spending all that money, for what?"

Manuel Travassos looked over at his daughter, proud of her inquisitive mind and her constant search for answers to the mystery of life's happenings.

"Ruth, you and the rest of you children have to keep in mind that God moves in mysterious ways to do things on behalf of all of us."

Nathan broke in and said, "I'm with Ruth. Only I agree with many of the farmers around here and others who work at the cannery. Why spend all that money when there are so many other things so much more important?"

Elizabeth spoke up, "Well, he's spent thousands, maybe millions of dollars, on the farm lots he's given us and our neighbors. It's about time someone did something for pastors, missionaries and YMCA workers, at least when it's time for them to retire."

Their father looked pleased at the children's response to what was happening around them, even though none of them was sure where all this was leading. He spoke up again, "I've heard Mr. Penney speak many times at meetings at Green Cove Springs and at the Agricultural Institute meetings. What makes him different from other wealthy businessmen is his interest in people and his love for them. He recently said that we are all living in hard times when we're discovering that our comfortable way of life has softened us and made us physically and spiritually flabby."

Asenath stood up and began to refill some of the empty cups while saying, "I hear you, Pa, but I still don't see how building that cathedral and all those luxurious apartments is going to make those people any better—their bodies or their souls."

Mrs. Travassos spoke up, "It's hard for us to see into the future but having all those acres to walk on, the golf course to play on, the pool to swim in, the many things to do together, is going to be good for those retiring, just like it is down at Moosehaven and other places that are being built. After all, Mr. Penney could have spent all that money on a big yacht or a mammoth mansion like the Vanderbilts."

"Ma's right," Rachel joined in, "I think it's wonderful that a man as wealthy as Mr. Penney is doing so much for others. And he's bringing in new families. Some of their children are in my class at school. I have new friends."

"That's what's happening," said Manuel Travassos, as he swatted a mosquito on the back of his neck. "Some of the ministers have already found a patch where they could plant potatoes and beans, and others are doing woodworking at the shop."

"And the big question that Mr. Franklin put to us," added María Travassos, "was, are we willing to become a part of the new community church and let our pastor serve a larger community?"

"I've talked a little with Rev. Mr. Conway," said her husband, "and he thinks that we ought to be at the dedication of the Memorial Home Community with open minds. Even though there are other farmers around here who want to keep to themselves. Our pastor feels Mr. Penney is doing all he can to widen and strengthen our Christian community. Any man who runs the risk of placing his money to that test must be within God's will."

"And the Travassos family will be at the dedication of the community, ready to do all we can to answer the invitation of Memorial Community Chapel," inserted María Travassos, as she lifted Job from the floor into her lap and hugged him warmly while she rocked him lovingly.

It was time for bed and each member of the family felt the importance of the decision awaiting their church. Anyway, they would all be at the dedication.

CHAPTER XI

THE DEDICATION OF A DREAM

IT WAS LATE AFTERNOON ON A SUNNY, COOLER THAN USUAL APRIL 22nd, 1927, when Joseph Cody, eleven-year-old son of Robert and Julia Cody stood at a big window overlooking the unfinished golf course which had cows on it, in the place of golfers.

The three Codys had moved into the newly built apartment at 302 Morton Drive located on the corner of Wilbanks Avenue. They had been there since November of 1926 waiting for the completion of other apartments and the new Memorial Home Chapel. Other families and couples had joined the new community as the dwelling places were completed.

The day had arrived when great things were about to happen. A recent shower gave the golf course the appearance of a green carpet covered with gleaming diamonds as the sun broke through the clouds.

Joseph watched with interest as some automobiles left Route 16 on the opposite side of the golf course and turned up Poling Boulevard which was still lined with piles of dirt and gravel where the workers had plowed a way to permit cars to enter. Joseph saw the cars bumping their way through the muddy puddles. He knew the cars were filled with people coming to the three-day dedicatory services but they were not his focus of interest. That was in the next building, to their right, which was located on the corner of Morton Drive and Poling Boulevard. It was where the Noblett family lived with their two children, Virginia and Roy. It was Virginia, the pretty teenaged daughter of this Texas family, who had captured the heart of Joseph.

Like the Codys, the Noblett family had moved into an upstairs apartment, after coming from Penmor Place in Green Cove Springs. These second floor apartments provided more space plus one additional small room, beyond what the downstairs apartments had, making it possible for their families to have children there.

The people living on the first floor, under the Cody family, were Mr. and Mrs. W.A. Wilson, retired YMCA workers who had no children. But Joseph wished it had been the Noblett family so that he and their son Roy could be closer buddies and also it would offer opportunities for him to be nearer to Virginia.

The Cody apartment was light and airy, with a large living room which had a fireplace in one corner, an alcove off that room with a Murphy bed where Rev. and Mrs. Cody slept, a dining room with windows overlooking Morton Boulevard on the golf course, a kitchenette off the dining room, and a small room on one side of the living room which was to be a laundry for the occupants. But Dr. Morton gave permission to use this as a small bedroom for Joseph. It had a cot, chair, small desk, and bookcase. The windows from that little room looked toward the Noblett cottage.

Julia Cody called to her boy as she emerged from the sleeping alcove in the one Sunday dress she owned, "Joseph, why are you standing there in that window, as though you had plenty of time to get dressed? We're supposed to be at the church in one hour and your father wants you to help him and the other men put up those chairs which are due to arrive from the Qui-Si-Sana Hotel."

Joseph growled to himself and started toward his room to put on his Sunday clothes. "I'm going, Mother, I just wanted to watch the cars come up Poling Boulevard and I think I saw the truck bring the chairs." Having said this, he secretly hoped the chairs would all be put up in the sanctuary of the chapel before he got there.

The day was an exciting one because it heralded the official opening of the Memorial Home Community which had been designed by Alan B. Mills, famous architect and builder from New Jersey. After struggling over which village style to adopt, he and Mr. Penney decided it would be French-Norman. Thus plans were made to build a rectangular village with the beautiful church at its center. The church tower would serve as the focal point of the community, as they did in the villages of France.

Mr. Mills hired Mr. Arthur Davis as his assistant who served as the expert in landscape designs. The two men directed the operation from an office located on the second floor of the Green Cove Springs National Bank.

Since the Cody family arrived at Long Branch, they had watched with amazement as the building project progressed. They saw the sixty acres, which were set aside as a memorial to Mr. Penney's father and mother, transformed from a flat, monotonous stretch of earth to a village of shapes and colors which attracted those driving past on their way to Starke. They marveled at the walls of solid concrete which were finished with stucco exteriors and painted with a soft bamboo color once they were topped with soft red-tiled roofs. The large windows, with screens, were trimmed with brown paint. Each building was built with different plans to avoid the monotony and provide relief from the flat landscape.

Joseph was dressed as his mother had requested but sat in a chair in his room peering at the window facing the west side of the Noblett cottage. His mother called to him behind his closed door.

"Do you have your room picked up? Remember, we may have visitors who will want to see what an upstairs apartment is like. We promised Dr. Morton we would be one of the model apartments for outsiders to look at."

"Aw shucks," growled Joseph, who was frustrated at not being able to see Virginia yet but also at the thought of having to sit through an organ concert when he'd rather stay in his room playing with his crystal set radio.

His mother, in the meantime, was thinking about the problems created by having a child in one of the apartments. She and Robert had discussed this many times after the Penney organization had opened the way for them to come to the new community even though Robert was not of retirement age. But, because of his health and the inability to serve a church effectively, the opening came for a temporary stay. The two of them felt that this was the way Mr. Penney would get his community going until it would have only retirees without children, or whose children already had left the nest.

Robert Cody burst through the downstairs front door and came hopping up the stairs, two at a time. He slipped into the kitchen area, and tiptoed up behind his wife and gave her a surprise hug. "Oh, darling, what a weekend this is going to be! I've just come from the Chapel and we can tell Joseph that the chairs are all up and he's not needed."

"He'll be glad to hear that. Frankly, Joseph has only one thing on his mind today and it's Virginia."

Her husband laughed. "We've got more on our minds than our son's romantic feelings," he said trying to focus his wife's attention on the reason for his enthusiasm. "I don't know why they're calling that church building the Chapel, it's really a cathedral! And look at this program booklet they gave me after we set up the chairs!" As he handed the booklet to Julia he continued, "When I stepped into that cathedral-like room and looked up at the Gothic arches, so high up, so beautiful, I thought I was in a huge cathedral in Europe! You get the feeling of awesome sacredness and Mrs. Foster was practicing on the new pipe organ which Ralph Gwinn gave in memory of his mother. What a sound, what music!"

Just then, Joseph came out of his room and as his mother

113

urged the two to sit down for the light meal she'd prepared, the boy said, "Papa, Mom says I have to go to the concert but I've got some homework to do. Can't I just stay here? I'll be at the big dedication on Sunday."

His father looked up at Julia and she slowly shook her head with a clear, "No," signal.

"Joseph," Robert Cody said, "you're young and I'm sure you don't realize the significance of the next few days but years from now you will look back on this day and tell your children, 'I was there with my father and mother and I not only heard the first concert on that beautiful pipe organ but I saw James C. Penney, the founder of the Penney stores.' You'll tell them about this dream of which we were a part, beginning at Green Cove Springs. You will be especially anxious to share the details of the second stage of that dream right here at Long Branch."

The boy puckered up his lips, not so much in protest about what his father said, but as a body signal which indicated that he knew his father was right, and besides, maybe Virginia would be there.

The first Dedicatory Service was held at 7:45 P.M. on Friday, April 22, 1927, with a crowded church and even an overflow into the social room off the left of the sanctuary. Folding doors had been opened and people sat all the way back to the door to the library which was already filling up with books.

Mr. Ralph Gwinn, attorney for the Penney Corporation and business associate of Mr. Penney, opened the service as he presided at the central pulpit located on a large, deeply-set platform with vases of all kinds of cut flowers lining the front. Chairs were occupied by several dignitaries, including the man who had had the dream and given much of his time, knowledge and money to see this day arrive. He sat closest to the pulpit and looked elegant in his new black suit, white shirt and bow tie. He had had his wavy white hair trimmed along with his distinguishing white mustache.

While Joseph Cody sat next to his parents, he acted very fidgety and kept scanning people to his left and right. His father leaned over and whispered, "She's three rows back, so why don't you just relax and enjoy this great moment."

Joseph gave an embarrassed smile and focused on Mr. Penney while Mrs. Foster played a stirring prelude. He noticed that the man seemed emotionally stirred. He sat with head bowed and kept wiping his eyes with his handkerchief. There was an attractiveness and radiance about him which impressed the boy. He wondered how it felt for the head of a great chain store like the J.C. Penney Corporation to be the one who thought of building a village and a church, and paying all the expenses.

Mr. Gwinn opened the service with a reminder of the historical significance of the event and then introduced the first speaker. He was Dr. William S. Starr, a professor from Princeton University and Joseph thought he was interesting. Then, Dr. Charles W. Flint, the chancellor of Syracuse University, spoke. Joseph didn't know what a "chancellor" was but it must have meant a man who uses big words.

At this point the boy sneaked a peek back at Virginia Noblett and she smiled at him. That made sitting through a boring speech worthwhile.

The next day, on Saturday, April 23, the Cody family decided that their son would not have to attend the banquet which was held at the Qui-Si-Sana Hotel in Green Cove Springs; Father would represent the family. Mother would stay home with Joseph while he did his homework for the next week.

The banquet was well attended by people from Long Branch, Green Cove Springs, Fleming Island, Middleburg, Orange Park, Jacksonville, Orlando, and Tallahassee, plus many out-of-state guests. They heard the Honorable John W. Martin, governor of the state of Florida; the Honorable Duncan V. Fletcher, Sr., senator to the U.S. Congress from Florida; the Honorable Raymond Robbins, famous travel lecturer; and Dr. Hamilton Holt, president of Rollins College in Orlando.

Mr. Penney told again the story of his mother and father and the powerful influences their Christ-like lives had upon him as he was growing up. He said, "I feel myself to be the humble instrument in the hands of God to carry on the work for which my parents gave their lives. What I have done and all that I have done is little enough when I think of what they did.

"Such measure of success as I may have achieved, and all that I am under God, I owe to my parents, to the depth of their faith, the unfaltering character of their influence and training, and the unfailing example they held ever before my eyes."

The audience was deeply moved by the power and depth of J.C. Penney's witness which acknowledged the impact of two devoted persons who were courageously willing to stand up for their convictions and at the same time to live out the humility and love of the Incarnate Christ.

The well-known writer and poetess Margaret E. Sangster read a poem which she wrote for the dedicatory occasion: "Perhaps They Did Not Know."

Perhaps they did not know when dusk was falling,
That in the days to be, their voices calling,
would aid uncounted, earthbound souls to rise.
Perhaps they did not know that their sure teaching
would lead a little boy up manhood's road,
until his tender hands, in kindness reaching,
have helped life's lonely ones to bear a load.
Perhaps they did not know! But very surely
as, in a lovely church, glad voices pray,
and as in homes old people dwell securely,
they know it now — will know it every day!
I think, for them, that Heaven's a sweeter place
because on earth — they left His peace and grace.

The next morning the Memorial Home Community gathered with other visitors in the Memorial Chapel to continue the great celebration.

They noted the interior of the new chapel with its sweeping arches, high front balcony with organ and choir, the tastefully leaded windows with simplistic designs, and the lovely chandeliers hanging from the Gothic heights. Someone was heard to say that the interior had electric amplifiers installed which were the first of their kind to be used in a public place.

Dr. Daniel Poling who presided over that service was identified in the program booklet as the director of the J.C. Penney Foundation. He led the congregation in singing the familiar hymns, "Holy, Holy, Holy," "O Worship the King" and "The Church's One Foundation," which were sung with an enthusiasm and spirit seldom heard in the average church. Dr. Francis B. Short, who was serving as a lecturer for the Penney Corporation, gave a rousing dedicatory sermon.

After the inspiring sermon, which was followed by special music, the dedicatory aspects of the celebration were presented. Mr. Penney was the first to speak as the donor of the community and the chapel. Among the words which he spoke were thoughts which many remembered later on. He said, "It is my earnest prayer that this ministry shall be an inspiration to others, that it shall not only bless those who live here, but that it shall become an example, the following of which shall enrich the whole Christian church and care for vast numbers beyond all those it may be possible for us to serve."

With the presentation of symbolic keys to the J.C. Penney Foundation, of which Dr. Poling was the chair, the Memorial Home Community and the Memorial Chapel were placed in the hands of that organization. Dr. G.K. Flack, president of the Residents Association and Mr.. Charles L. Rood, treasurer of the J.C. Penney Foundation, gave addresses of acceptance. After the service the people gathered outside the chapel where tables and chairs had been set up on the circle by the front stairs.

The Cody family saw the Noblett family sitting next to the Rev. and Mrs. Layport, one of the early retired couples who had arrived at Penmor Place the winter before. The Codys joined them and Joseph was delighted to find a chair next to Virginia.

Mr. Layport waved to Mr. and Mrs. Wilson, the downstairs neighbors of the Codys, and indicated that they had some chairs available. As the Wilsons proceeded to join the cluster, the Rev. and Mrs. Emmett Stevens, newly retired missionaries from China, followed them to take the last chairs without occupants in the cluster.

In the opposite direction of this group sat Mr. and Mrs. Manuel Travassos with their eight children. Others from the Bordenville Community Church had joined them.

As people went to the punch bowl, set up on a center table, Mr. Layport and Mr. Wilson began serving the folk in their circle with cups of fruit juice and platters of food. While they were each munching on the tasty sandwiches, Mr. Noblett felt led to get better acquainted with the Stevenses.

"Tell us a little about what it was like for the two of you to live in China."

"Well, it's pretty hard to do with all this crowd milling about and talking, but we'll be happy to answer any specific questions you might have," responded the Rev. Mr. Stevens.

With this, Roy Noblett leaned forward and said, "Tell us about the Chinese bandits over there. Did you ever see any?"

Mrs. Stevens spoke up, while noting her husband had a mouthful of food, "We never were captured by bandits but we did have missionary friends who were. They were not molested or harmed but the bandits were seeking a ransom payment."

"Did they get it?" Virginia asked eagerly, and the two missionaries began to explain why those things happened and how the friends were finally released.

Joseph entered into the dialogue with the couple and the other families.

Mrs. Cody leaned over to her husband and whispered, "I'm glad Joseph is discovering how intriguing this community is with such a fascinating variety of older people living right here with the rest of us."

"Yes," agreed her husband, "and it occurs to me that even with the Wilsons living downstairs we haven't had much opportunity to find out about their work with the YMCA."

The people gathered in the various clusters were having a good time with conversations and laughter filling the warm tropical air. Then a signal was given by one of the leaders and they all began to enter the church for the 2:30 P.M. service.

After an organ prelude, the congregation was invited by Dr. D. Walter Morton, their beloved superintendent since the first residents arrived at Green Cove Springs, to stand and sing the Doxology. This was followed by a major address by Mr. John H. Perry, president of the American Press Association. He was followed by addresses of thirteen retired ministers who had come to the new community. They each represented a major denomination and promised to give a "short speech," but as Manuel Travassos said to his wife, "those preachers don't know what the word 'short' means."

Everyone present, including some squirming children, was struck by the demonstration of the ecumenical nature of the Memorial Home Community and the sharpness of most of the preachers, in spite of their ages.

Margaret E. Sangster, in writing an article for the *Christian Herald* (May 14, 1927), pointed out that the words of the ministers affected her more than anything else during that service. She wrote, "It was the afternoon service, however—during which thirteen different members of the community spoke—that most deeply stirred me. Thirteen old men representing thirteen different denominations. Men who had preached in tiny hamlets, men who had spoken God's Holy Word; in city homes of prayer, men who had been missionaries and men who had been circuit riders. Working for the love of a blessed Savior rather than for monetary gain."

With all that had happened since 10:30 A.M., the celebration was still not over. Next, was the dedication of the new Aeolian organ which began with a recital at seven o'clock. Miss Bertha Foster, the director of the Miami Conservatory of Music, played "The Bells of St. Anna de Beaupre" by Russell, "Largo" from Dvorak's New World Symphony, plus four other smaller pieces.

The seven-thirty actual dedication of the organ was led by Dr. Burdette Lewis, the vice president of the Penney-Gwinn Corporation. After a speech from Dr. Lemuel Martin, the president of De Pauw University, Mr. Ralph Gwinn presented the organ as a memorial to his mother. Then, an address of acceptance was given by Dr. Francis Short, the Methodist pastor who influenced J.C. Penney on his pilgrimage of spiritual growth, when the younger Mr. Penney began to form his chain of department stores.

As the three-day celebration closed on Sunday night, the residents were exhausted but, at the same time, were exhilarated by the mountaintop experiences. It was an event never to be forgotten, especially the presence of Mr. Penney and the essence of the words he spoke. One thought was lifted up by newspapers and magazines all over the country: "Beyond all the investments that I have made, this investment has already yielded me a return in satisfaction that I have found nowhere else. And so today, with a mind full of sacred memories, memories that remain though the ones calling them forth have passed from this life into the better and larger life beyond, I give these buildings...as a place where men and women who followed Christ may live out their lives for the holy cause for which my parents lived and died."

So, in memory of the Rev. James Cash Penney and his beloved wife, Mary Frances Penney, their famous son had set the direction, through his philanthropic gifts, of a Christian retirement community which was unique and enduring.

The following day those who gathered at the post office to pick up their mail were sharing their feelings about the significance of the previous days. Mr. Noblett sat on a bench in a corner reading a letter he had opened. As Robert Cody stepped into the post office his friend got up and approached him, "I have a life-changing letter in my hand, Bob, which informs me that the conference has a good church in Texas where it wants me to serve."

"You mean, you'd leave us to go back there, now that you're nicely settled in your new apartment?"

"We only came until there was an opening for me and when my wife was feeling better."

"I realize that," answered Cody, "after hearing those retired men yesterday I was reminded that this place was built for them."

"Yes, and now that we know what it's like down here we can return when we retire, without the children," he added.

At the noon meal Robert Cody shared with his wife and Joseph the news about the Noblett family returning to Texas. Joseph was devastated. Little did he guess that his father would make a move back to Tennessee within three months.

His wife summed it up as they were preparing to move, "We've been privileged to be in a little bit of heaven and now we move aside to make a place for others to have the same love, joy and fellowship that we've known."

CHAPTER XII

THE GREAT STRUGGLE

IT WAS THE KIND OF JUNE DAY THAT POETS WRITE ABOUT AND artists paint, as James and Caroline Penney sat on the large veranda at their home in White Plains, New York.

Their two girls, Carol Marie and Mary Frances, were playing with dolls on the further end of that porch. They were totally unaware of the dark cloud which had engulfed their father.

The parents were rocking slowly in the rocking chairs which they had brought up from Florida. Neither said a word for a long time. All that could be heard above the creaking of their chairs was the chirping of birds in the trees and the happy exchange between the two girls as they played "Mommy and Daddy" with their dolls.

"Jimmy," said Caroline, lovingly, "you've just got to snap out of it. You're taking this Depression too personally. It's killing you, it's affecting our marriage, and I'm sure it's doing more to the girls than we realize."

"Too seriously?" he uttered with a tone of disgust. "I'm not blaming myself for what happened to our economy in 1929, but having to sell our place in Florida and coming here to White Haven and closing all the rooms but two is serious for you and the girls. How do you think I feel about laying off the men who kept up these fifty acres and causing their families to suffer? Think of what's happening to the people who lost everything at City National Bank in Miami when I was the one who had invested and lost the money they were depending on? That's enough to cause anyone to jump out of the office window."

"I married you not for the millions you had but because I loved you and you loved me. So, we lost forty million dollars. Think about what we have left, which can never be measured in dollars."

"I know that. I tell myself that every time I look in the mirror or try to pray. But the cloud still covers my mind and soul. Just this week I've asked Ralph Gwinn to go to Penney Farms and tell the people at the agricultural center and the Memorial Home Community that I can no longer be their benefactor. All my support potential is gone!"

"You've still got the *Christian Herald* and those projects related to it, and the farm project seems to be going well, especially at the Foremost Dairies. And just this week you heard that the number of residents at the Memorial Home Community is increasing."

"I've borrowed seven million dollars more, putting up all my stocks as collateral, and I've asked the Penney Corporation to put me on their payroll for the first time ever.

I've asked Ralph Gwinn to make sure that my going bankrupt will not affect the Retirement Community and I've asked
Foremost Dairies to take over, completely, the farms. And
that's putting people out of work. The Memorial Community
people are going to have to pay a maintenance fee and most
of them can't afford that. They have no retirement resources.
What if my father and mother were there? They'd have to
move somewhere else. What is this going to do to all those
servants of God I promised free living quarters and a happy
retirement?"

"But, Jimmy, you've done what you thought was right
and the will of God. Nothing can separate you from His
strength and power. He will see you through!"

"You sound like your old boss, the bishop, but no matter
how much I preach that to myself, it's just words, words,
words! And the dark tunnel I'm in gets longer and darker all
the time!"

"Let's go out into the garden, darling, it will make you
feel better. The girls will be all right here while they keep on
playing." With this she took her husband's hand and walked
with him out into the gardens. What J.C. Penney was going
through was shared by countless millions in those terrible
years following 1929 when the Great Depression put so many
people out of work and tested their faith and endurance.

Up until that time, things had gone well for James C.
Penney. More stores had been added to his chain. He had
been asked to be the president of the *Christian Herald* magazine. He was named the chairman of the City National Bank
in Miami. He became the largest depositor and investor in

that institution. Filled with the exhilaration of success, neither he nor others suspected the oncoming of the disastrous economic slump.

Mr. Penney had attracted attention worldwide, not only because of his genius in creating a new concept of merchandising, but because of his farm experiment at Long Branch, Florida, which seemed to offer hope for struggling farmers, and the creation of a new kind of retirement community which was a memorial to his mother and father. When his books appeared called, *My Experience with the Golden Rule* (1949); *Fifty Years with the Golden Rule* (1950); *Lines of a Layman* (1956); and *View from the Ninth Decade* (1960), plus two books written in collaboration with others, *J.C. Penney, the Man with a Thousand Partners* and *Main Street Merchant*, invitations swamped his mailbox as people and organizations wanted him as their speaker. A number of newspapers around the country, plus a feature article in *The Saturday Evening Post* magazine added to all this.

Many of the ventures he took with a selfless motivation for service to others began to undermine his financial security in the late 20's. There is little doubt that the millions he put into the farm experiment as well as spending two million dollars to build the Memorial Home Community had drained his cash reserves. All of this was happening while he was pouring money into the *Christian Herald* magazine and the International Society of Christian Endeavor, an ecumenical youth movement which affected many young lives. He also contributed to vocational guardian efforts in private colleges and supported the Judson Health Center, which was founded to deal with the effects of malnutrition and rickets.

It was estimated that J.C. Penney during the course of one year personally helped over 100 organizations which had a mission-to-people purpose. As people learned of his generosity and mission concern for others, he was in increasing demand as a speaker which gave him the opportunity to witness to his belief in the relationship between his Christian convictions and his daily work.

In his book, *Fifty Years with the Golden Rule*, which was published in 1950, Mr. Penney refers to the black period between 1929-1932. He wrote:

"As the depression deepened, from time to time some commercial loans in the bank portfolio became unsatisfactory to the bank examiners. None of them was connected with me personally nor with J.C. Penney Company, or the Penney-Gwinn Corporation. Several times I took out slow or unacceptable loans, substituting cash; it amounted to hundreds of thousands of dollars. I continued borrowing on my personal stock holdings to do it. My confidence in my own financial invulnerability was complete. I borrowed more millions to put into the needs of the *Christian Herald*, the Memorial Home Community, the Penney Farm Project, the National Youth Radio, the Emmadine Farm and the Foremost Dairy Products, Inc.

"Stock prices, in general, began a strange downward plunge. Banks called their loans. The panic lasted not days, but years."

Recognizing that he was, as he put it, "flat broke," he quickly deeded the sixty acres with all its buildings to the

Memorial Home Society (which after his death was renamed "The Penney Retirement Community"). The right for the residents to govern themselves, with a board set up by Mr. Penney, was granted by Mr. Penney.

At the same time that he gave up control of his retirement community, he deeded his share in the *Christian Herald* magazine to Dr. Daniel Poling, who was at that time the president of the Penney Foundation.

The farm project, with the Agricultural Institute and the one hundred farms which had been established in the Long Branch area, were put under the Foremost Dairies. They closed out the Institute and abandoned all other aspects of the farm project which depended upon Mr. Penney's financial support.

While he was broken in body and in spirit, the following years proved his gifts and labors had not been in vain.

The Memorial Home Community lost a large number of its residents when they were informed that they would no longer be supported by Mr. Penney's benevolence. However, within a year, new people took their places and at that time they had ninety residents living in the cottages.

Dr. Morton, their local leader since 1925, was called to head up Syracuse University and he was succeeded by Dr. William A. Willson, who managed the post-Depression problems and proceeded to make some changes, including the providing of health care with a doctor on campus. Dr. George P. Hammer came to the community and set up a medical practice assisted by several retired nurses living in the cottages.

The Penney Memorial Church began to thrive. It invited

the new community church, organized by the farm families who had come to Long Branch in 1925 and met in a building provided by the farm project, to join the new church as an expression of their ecumenical unity.

The Bordenville Community Church was also invited to join the Penney Memorial Church which they voted to do. A large congregation filled the Penney Church and a thriving Sunday School met every Sunday.

The Rev. George Hall was called to be the pastor of the Memorial Church and the Penmor Residents Association appointed a committee to direct the affairs of the church.

The president of the Association, the Rev. Robert Cody, and the members of the Residents Association adopted as its objective: "The cultivation of a more intimate acquaintance, the uniting of all the members into a close bond of fellowship and the promotion of the physical, social and spiritual welfare of all." The makeup of the resident body of the retirement community was of people from thirty-two states and Canada. They represented sixteen denominations.

By 1935 Mr. Penney had emerged from the trials of bankruptcy, chiefly through the profits of his dairy projects in various parts of the country, propelled by Emmadine Farm and the Foremost Dairies. He returned frequently to the retirement community which meant so much to him.

The Penney Memorial Church planned a big celebration to fete Mr. Penney and they called it a "Love Feast." The farm project also continued on under its own momentum and in 1936 had a celebration of its 10th anniversary. A pilgrimage of farmers came to that event from all over the country.

World War II was on the horizon when, in 1940, the *Christian Herald* took over the Memorial Home Community as an adjunct to their mission involvements. By doing this, the magazine was able to tell the Memorial Home story, creating support and new residents. This arrangement continued for nineteen years with Dr. Poling as the inspiring leader. Under his leadership he helped bring about many needed repairs and other changes in the community's life.

Mr. Penney was happy to see the retirement community being renewed and attracting new residents under an altered administration pattern.

A big part of the renewal was the *Christian Herald*'s campaign to raise one million dollars to build a 100-apartment facility for single residents. It was called the Christian Herald Quadrangle and became the largest building on the campus. It had the same French-Norman design of the other buildings and included a lovely dining room, library, and administrative offices. It was built around a broad courtyard with walks, gardens and trees.

Later, the first medical facility was built through the financial help of the Olin family. It was named the Mary Olin Clinic. Dr. Poling gave tireless effort to see these improvements carried out as he served as the president of the Memorial Home Board of Directors.

Eventually the *Christian Herald* felt the need of divesting itself of all financial responsibility for the retirement community. It gave up the administrative responsibilities also and helped form a new Board of Directors made up of people willing to give voluntary service to the community.

With J.C. Penney as their personal model, the residents themselves began to take more responsibility for the management and maintenance of the community. Around this same time the Board opened up the community to all laypeople who had a desire to retire in a Christian community where the ideals of Mr. Penney would be carried out.

The founder of the community continued on the Board of Directors and saw all that he had done weather the storm of World War II, when army and navy personnel were put up in some of the cottages. He also knew of the arrival of Hurricane Dora in 1964. Though palm trees were uprooted and blown down, the well-built buildings, cottages, quadrangle, and Mary Olin Clinic stood the test, emerging without damage.

An Arts and Crafts Center was built, which was made possible by a generous gift given by A. Richard Diebold, a member of the Board of Directors. At this time the whole idea of volunteerism emerged as a central program in running the community.

Mr. Penney continued to write and speak during the years following his struggle through the Depression. He told of his learning through suffering and struggle. He emphasized that a person would be a failure in life if he or she was known only for the possession of financial security. He shared his concern over the materialistic age in which all were living. He confessed that the biggest mistake he had made was thinking that the achievement of success and wealth would give him all that he needed in life.

Many times he spoke of the great struggle that almost broke him in health and spirit, as it left him with far less money than what he had before he was led to the great discovery that God had plans for him. Plans which would lead him to a peace of mind and an inner security which he had not known fully.

In speaking, as part of the national laymen's movement, he talked about his new discoveries through prayer. He admitted that for a long time he had instinctively relied upon himself for the strength and power to go forward. But, more and more, prayer became his main source of light and strength. He refused to suggest any one method of prayer and believed a pattern could evolve in each life according to our individual personalities and needs.

It was his practice to have a number of books at his bedside which he turned to before going to sleep. Among them was the Bible, but he liked writers like Frank Laubach, Samuel Shoemaker, and John Fifield. He said they helped open up fresh spiritual vistas which helped him learn, not only about spirituality, but how to give one's self over to "being spiritual." It was the seeking of God's will and the presence of Jesus Christ that made the difference in his life when he went through good times and times of struggle.

CHAPTER XIII

MATTERS OF THE SPIRIT

IT WAS DURING THE LATE THIRTIES THAT MR. PENNEY SPOKE TO AN audience of student teachers. It happened in the Normal School in Chillicothe, Missouri. His topic was, "The Application of Christian Principles in the Business World."

Only the day before he had visited the old homestead farm where he grew up as a boy and had purchased once he became a millionaire. He named it the Home Place. It was his way of preserving the memory of his father and mother.

As he sat on the platform of the Normal School auditorium he must have had strange thoughts about what had taken place in his own life even though he never went to a college. He looked down into the faces of the young people and saw expressions of anticipation. After all, they were about to hear from one, who like them, had great ambitions but never really expected to achieve the goals he had in mind.

After he was given a glowing introduction by the school president he seemed to radiate a calm, assured presence which affected even the most disinterested of the future teachers.

He opened his remarks by reminding them that he was not an orator, nor a preacher. Then he said: "Though I've told you I am not a preacher, it may surprise you to hear me say that I have chosen a Scripture text for my address to you today. It comes directly from the lips of the Master of Galilee who said, 'Render unto Caesar the things that are Caesar's and unto God the things that are God's.'

"If there were any preachers here today, they would probably not feel that this was a proper text to introduce a message to a body of normal school future teachers, but I am using these words because I think it is wrong to separate the sacred and the secular. That's why I think I should say at the outset that I do not believe the affairs of the business world should be separated from the matters of the spirit.

"I am not advocating that one should apply his or her personal theology to one's work, whether a businessperson or a school teacher. However, what I am suggesting is that God should be the center of one's life.

"Whatever our Christian beliefs we should always be motivated by the desire to achieve the maximum best in terms of ethics and relationships. It is my personal conviction that the maximum best comes from knowing God's will and obeying it.

"Too many people today try to achieve material success by whatever means without thought of what God has revealed in His Word or without understanding the teaching of the Golden Rule.

"Since I began with my first Golden Rule store in Kemmerer, Wyoming, I have tried to demonstrate honesty, fairness, initiative, and quality in all my relationships, whether as co-workers or as customers.

"As you no doubt know I have achieved such success. But, I want you to know that becoming a millionaire is not enough...no...it's more than that, it's a matter of discovering the things of the spirit.

"For some of you it may sound as though I'm preaching, as my father did so well many years ago, in Hamilton, just up the road. But, I want to tell you it was his life, not just his words, that led me on a journey of searching for the highest and the best.

"The secret of my father's life and my mother's life was the way they imitated the Master by giving of themselves with selflessness and sacrifice. At no time were they motivated by money profit but always by the benefits they shared with others. They never separated the secular from the sacred. As God motivated people they received blessings no money could buy and they left blessings upon all whom they touched."

Then Mr. Penney gave a moving testimony about how God had touched his life at certain times during his walk through the years. He told of the influence of his wives and his pastors. He also recounted the story of his despondency in New York City and his being drawn to the mission in the Bowery. He graphically told of being driven to his knees by the life of the man who had gone through the same things he was experiencing and had found that surrender to the Master was his release.

At the close of the talk the president opened up a time of questions and dialogue between Mr. Penney and the students. One young woman, sitting toward the front, stood and asked the speaker where he had his church membership.

Mr. Penney stepped up to the lectern and paused for what seemed to be a long time and then in a halting, stammering manner said, "I didn't tell you about an experience I had almost ten years ago. It happened in Battle Creek, Michigan, where I was scheduled to speak at a noon luncheon of prominent business leaders. However, I was not psychologically or spiritually ready for such an occasion.

"Some of you may be too young to remember well the devastating effects of the Great Depression but, at that time, I was at my peak in terms of business success and material wealth. The depression wiped me out. Banks where I had placed millions of dollars went broke. The farms and Institute for Agricultural Studies in Florida, which I established and where I invested a large portion of my money to help farmers, were closed down. I had to get rid of many of my properties and even close down a part of my home in White Plains, New York, while I struggled to save the Memorial Home Retirement Center I had established in Florida for clergy, YMCA workers and missionaries.

"All this sent me into a valley of depression. I could not sleep at night. I could not eat during the day. I was experiencing a nervous breakdown as I felt God had abandoned me...I thought seriously of committing suicide as the easiest way out of all this.

"I was going through what later reading helped me see,

the Dark Nights of the Soul: the ancient mystics first wrote about this.

"And would you believe? In this condition I was scheduled to speak to laymen sharing good news and giving them a spiritual lift!"

With this he stopped speaking, took out a large white handkerchief and wiped his eyes and mustache. Looking at the young woman who had asked the question about membership in a local church he said, "I'm giving you an answer that's longer than what you may have wanted but I think it important to share my experience because each of you may have the same spiritual struggle.

"I never became a member of a local church because of the poor treatment given my father by the Hamilton church when they fired him as their pastor after a painful business meeting where they accused him of heresy. I witnessed that as a boy!

"Thereafter," he continued to an entranced audience, "I attended various churches, sought counsel from wonderful men and women of God, while still having dark walks in the valleys and times of mountaintop joy...always struggling over the question of full commitment of my life to the God and Christ of my childhood.

"While visiting Battle Creek, I was once again at the end of my rope. My business world had tumbled, my communication with my colleagues, my friends, and even my wife and children had broken down.

"Then, this luncheon appointment with Dr. Elmer Eggleston, an old school friend from my high school days in

Hamilton, came up while I was in Battle Creek for the speaking engagement. He was a member of the Kellogg Sanitarium medical staff."

He added with a smile, "All that cereal you people ate from Kellogg packages helped put that sanitarium there to help meet my needs.

"The doctor looked at me as we met in the restaurant and said, 'My Lord, Jim, what's wrong with you...you look terrible!'

"I told him that when I finally struggled out of bed that same morning I found my body had broken out with what he later diagnosed as shingles.

"He insisted on canceling my speaking engagement and placing me in the sanitarium. I didn't have the heart to tell the doctor I was broke and wouldn't be able to pay him or the hospital." Mr. Penney told the students how he was sedated for a long period of time. The escape into oblivion was welcomed as a merciful deliverance from his psychological and physical pain.

He felt that his life was at its end. However, he began to think of his wife, Caroline, who was home with the children struggling with her own problems. He got up, began to write letters during the night, then went back to sleep and woke up with the morning sun streaming into his room.

At this point in his story, Mr. Penney looked at his watch, turned to the president and said, "I really must not finish my story, I'm taking too much time...."

The president waved his hand and said, "We want to hear it, Mr. Penney, we still have some time and besides the students

are waiting expectantly to the answer about church membership."

"Thank you, you're all very patient, and I will get to that
in a moment...

"That morning in Battle Creek, when I awoke I realized I
was alive! That was a surprise to me! There must have been a
reason for God staying with me and bringing me through.

"I dressed and went downstairs to have my first breakfast
in several days only to find that it was too early for the dining room to be opened.

"Stealing quietly along the corridor towards the stairs
leading to my room, I heard the soothing sounds of a very
familiar hymn. It was one I sang many times while sitting
with my mother and family in church.

'Be not dismayed whate'er betides,

God will take care of you...

All you need He will provide...

God with take care of you...'

"I headed toward that singing like a lost chick seeking the
protection of the mother hen's wings. Through a door I saw
the interior of a little chapel. I entered. A small group of doctors, nurses, and patients were worshiping.

"Someone read a portion of Scripture as I slipped into a
back pew. 'Come unto me, all you that are heavy laden and I
will give you rest.' This was followed by a time of prayer as
several participants offered spoken petitions.

"At that time something happened to me which I've
never been able to explain or describe. It was a life-changing
miracle and I have been a different man ever since. I saw God

in all His glory and planned to be baptized and join a church."

What he didn't tell the students that day was that the Battle Creek transformation had taken place ten years before and he still had not joined a church or been baptized.

Since the Christmas Day, two weeks after the Battle Creek mountaintop experience, when he returned home with his family, James Penney showed a different style of living and a renewed personality which had everyone talking about the changes in his life.

From that time forward, James Cash Penney sought every means to tell his story of being touched by God and lifted to new levels of service to others.

He emphasized in his extensive speaking tours that it was easier to give of one's money than to give of one's self.

He wrote articles in the *Christian Herald*, *Guideposts*, and other periodicals. He spoke at national assemblies, summer conferences, denominational conventions and ecumenical gatherings. He received honorary degrees and awards galore. He spoke in small and large churches of all denominations.

From that time forward, perhaps because of his advancing years, because he was sincerely seeking God's will for his life, J.C. Penney struggled over the question of baptism and church membership. He had long discussions with Daniel Poling, who was sensitive to his dilemma, and he also talked frequently with his wife, Caroline, who patiently waited for his decision. While in Chillicothe, Missouri, he was invited to speak at the Christian Church (Disciple) and was shocked to discover they had communion at every service. In his book, *Fifty Years with the Golden Rule,* he tells how embarrassed he was as he told the pastor that he had never partaken of communion before. The pastor responded by asking him if he thought he was a Christian. Penney answered with a resolute "yes." The pastor then insisted he should participate in the service. During that significant service the Spirit of the Lord touched Penney and he decided that he would be baptized. That same night he phoned his wife and told her he had decided to be baptized and to join the church.

On Easter Sunday, April 5, 1942, a fascinating drama took place in the living room of the manse of the Baptist Temple on Broad Street, Philadelphia.

The distinguished pastor, Dr. Daniel Poling, still dressed in his gray cutaway coat with striped pants, white shirt and black tie, stood next to his wife, Lillian, who wore an exquisite pink Easter dress with a corsage still pinned to her bosom.

"This is turning out to be one of the most memorable Easters of my ministry," said Dr. Poling, as he spoke to the others standing in the large living room with its brightly-colored oriental rug and elegant pieces of furniture that the globe-trotting pastor and wife had acquired during their world travels.

"A few weeks ago, while we were visiting the Memorial Home Community in Florida, my friend and associate, J.C. Penney, asked me to baptize him."

"How wonderful!" exclaimed Mary Sweet, wife of the Rev. George Sweet, Associate Pastor of the Baptist Temple. She reached out and grabbed Penney's hand.

"We've been waiting a long time. When will this happen?" she questioned.

Penney looked at Poling as if to ask if this was a question he should answer or the pastor?

With an affirmative nod from the pastor, the answer came from Mr. Penney.

"For too many years I have struggled over full commitment to Jesus Christ through Christian baptisms. Because of what happened to my father by baptized people in Hamilton, Missouri, I was determined not to join the ranks of church hypocrites.

"Then as the years passed, God kept tugging at my soul and though I resisted the pull by making excuses, including the idea that at my stage in life some would interpret my act of baptism as a publicity stunt rather than a time of surrender.

"Some time ago I came close to joining the Penney Memorial Church, but I kept searching for ways to be baptized without it being flashed on national news as a twisted public relations move."

He stopped and turned to his wife, Caroline, who was beginning to shed some tears. She reached out and hugged him while Dr. Poling spoke: "I offered to baptize Mr. Penney in the privacy of our home with just the six of us present. I also remember our talking together at Penney Farms about doing this and told him about an eighty-nine-year-old man who was baptized."

J.C. Penney broke in, "And what got to me was your telling me that old gentleman had said, 'Jesus was immersed and I wish to be as much like Jesus as it's possible for me to be!' And that's why I decided to be baptized, too!"

"The word from my husband filled me with an incredible joy," added Caroline Penney. "I prayed daily for him as he struggled to make a decision."

"Yes," responded her husband, "here I'm married to a baptized Episcopalian, and asking my close friend, a baptized Baptist preacher, to baptize me—even contrary to his church's way of doing it—in private."

Dr. Poling smiled and said, "I think my deacons will understand for we all know it's not the amount of water that makes the difference but the depth of the meaning of the act. And, as I think of it, the time Jesus was baptized was probably as private as this."

With this the pastor signaled to Mrs. Poling and she brought a silver bowl from the kitchen while the participants were seated and she handed it to Mr. Sweet.

Then Dr. Poling had J.C. Penney kneel on a small pillow which he took off the sofa and placed in the middle of the oriental rug. The associate held the bowl in front of Penney and offered a prayer of invocation asking the presence and blessing of God.

Poling put his hands in the water and gently sprinkled some on the bowed man's head.

"I baptize you, James Cash Penney, in the name of the Father..."

Then he dipped his hand a second time and sprinkled Penney's head and intoned, "I baptize you in the name of the Son..."

And finally, with a third sprinkling of water, he said, "and I baptize you in the name of the Holy Spirit...."

Then he prayed, "O God, our loving and wonderful Lord, on this significant Easter Sunday we have witnessed the baptism of your child, James Cash Penney. We rejoice that it is happening on the day we celebrate the resurrection of our Lord Jesus. We also rejoice that it symbolizes the rising that has taken place in the life of your servant, James.

"We confess before the mystery of your miraculous love that there is much we do not understand, yet we also offer our praises because You take us as we are.

"We praise You for the way You have walked with our beloved friend, through dark valleys and triumphant times. How we thank You for the impact of his life and service.

"Fill him with your Spirit. Sustain him with your strength. Use him through your love. In the name of Jesus Christ, our risen Savior. Amen."

There wasn't a dry eye in the manse living room as James C. Penney stood up straight, feeling a burden had been lifted and a high day of spiritual filling had been experienced. He had reached a mountaintop in his spiritual journey.

It was eight years later, at the age of seventy-five, that J.C. Penney finally conquered the feeling he had originally had about church membership. On May 14, 1950, Mr. Penney became a member of Penney Memorial Church at Penney Farms, Florida.

Dr. Poling accompanied him to the church and joined in giving him the right hand of fellowship after preaching a stirring sermon.

The spiritual climb of James Cash Penney had reached a new peak. He had hurdled the obstacles of the years, and felt that his mother and father were smiling down upon him.

CHAPTER XIV

YOUNG AT 95

A LARGE GROUP OF MEN AND WOMEN, WITH CUPS IN HAND AND plates with assorted cookies on their laps, sat patiently while the chattering sound of conversations filled the reception room of the American Bible Society headquarters located on Broadway, next to Lincoln Center, in New York City.

They had come with excited anticipation, for the first publication announcement of the latest version of the Bible was to be made. It was called, *Good News for Modern Man*, and it was to be presented to James Cash Penney upon the occasion of his recently celebrated ninety-fifth birthday.

The local staff, district secretaries from all over the United States, friends and co-workers of Mr. Penney, plus some of his children and grandchildren, and a large number of the news media, applauded as the smartly dressed Mr. Penney was escorted to the front. He looked as distinguished as ever with his flowing white hair and neatly-trimmed white mustache. They noticed he had put on a little weight and walked with a cane.

After presenting Mr. Penney, the president of the society said, "Mr. Penney, we have invited you here to make the presentation of the *Good News for Modern Man*, a new 1971 pictorial edition, because you have embodied that Good News in your business and in your personal relationships with people. We honor the fact that you learned the precepts of the Word from your parents and through the long uphill struggle of your life, you were faithful to the teachings put in your hands at an early age.

"We also celebrate not only your ninety-five years of life, but the dedication you showed in spreading the Good News to modern people here at home and also abroad."

Then he was presented a white leather-bound copy of the *Good News for Modern Man*, 1971 version, amidst the cheers and clapping of those present.

While cameras flashed, he stood waiting for the quiet to come and then, in words dripping with emotion, he said, "This is one of the greatest honors of my life and I want to promise to you that, even at ninety-five, I will continue to study the Book which has meant so much to me during my life. And I assure you I will continue to be learning from it, with the hope that it will help me to be a better man.

"I also want to tell you of how much joy and peace I have received from the Word of God which shares the certainty of the daily and everlasting love and power of Jesus Christ, our Lord."

As one looks at the pilgrimage of the ninety-five years which Mr. Penney experienced, it becomes apparent that the road he traveled was not that which was commonly thought of by the traditional church. Though he was born into a Christian family where his father and mother served sacrificially in a small Missouri church which treated them cruelly and left scars on him that he bore for the rest of his life, J.C. Penney was never able to escape from that influence.

Most Christians of that day in which he emerged had an experience of Christian conversion, either of a sudden, cataclysmic change or, of a gradual slow process, which enabled them to discover what it meant to live out the Christian style in the world.

J.C. Penney reversed the process and resisted an admittance of conversion or even the joining of a Christian church. Instead he brought the ethics of the Bible and the lifestyle intended for all church members into his business. Though there were skeptics who laughed at his attempt to foster partnership in his stores and the Golden Rule as the precept to follow, he proved that what God taught him through his Christian parents could bring success to his business endeavors.

He rejected the use of piety manifested in the extreme and set out to prove that partnership, mutual respect and the carrying out of a high ethical practice in his business could be one way to follow God's will. So, for him, action came first.

Then, later in life, he experienced a conversion which led to a closer walk with God and a desire to become more philanthropic in reaching out to people with special needs. Thus, his establishment of the Agricultural Institute and farms for the sake of farmers. As he often said, "Farmers and faith can be one." Then, his concern for retired elderly clergy, missionaries and YMCA workers, resulted in the building of the

Penney Retirement Community at Penney Farms, Florida, and his creation of a model retirement environment.

The famous author, cleric and educator, Dr. Frank Meads, visited the Penney Retirement people in 1944 and wrote, "I found myself sitting, talking, eating, laughing, worshiping, playing golf, and enjoying life with the happiest crowd in the world."

Dr. Kenneth Wilson, former editor of the *Christian Herald* magazine and presently a resident of Penney Retirement Community, said, "J.C. Penney's passion was for people more than making money."

The actions of Mr. Penney in attempting to relate the meaning of the Gospel to all areas of life was manifested in his involvement with youth and caught the attention of the country and those who tried to reach out to the young and the old.

There is a mural painted by the eminent muralist Dean Fausell. It hangs in the lobby of the J. C. Penney Hall at the National 4-H Club Center in Washington, D.C. As one looks at it, Mr. Penney can be seen, with a Golden Rule store painted as the background, embracing a young man who has a calf at his side. All around are other young people who represent the 4-H Clubs everywhere. They hold their baskets of vegetables and fruits. At their sides are hens, chickens, lambs and pets, while they grip their rakes and hoes ready for action. They represent the spirituality of the man in their midst who is happy to see that spiritual dynamic translated into lives dedicated to the enhancement of farm life.

In looking at the spiritual journey of Mr. Penney, it is

important to note the influences of the women he married.

Berta Alva Hess was the practical, down-to-earth, hard-working mother of his first two children who served unselfishly as the first employee of his first store. Though she was limited in terms of formal education, she had a strong desire to put God into their family life. It was she who introduced him to Dr. Francis Short who, in turn, became a spiritual advisor and guide to the couple.

Mary Hortense Kimball added a new dimension to her husband's life when her education at Bryn Mawr and her special interest in the arts opened up J.C. Penney's horizons to the place of writing, speaking, and knowing good music. She, too, added a spiritual dimension to their family only to be cut off by death three years later. Once again Penney was struck by the untimely death of a talented and beautiful wife who left a little boy, Kimberly, to be brought up by his father.

Caroline Bertha Authenreith was J.C. Penney's third wife. She was twenty years younger than he and she was married to him for forty-five years. With her youthful zest for life and her involvement in the inner workings of the Methodist Episcopal church, she brought a new vitality to her husband and may have been the one who finally persuaded him to be baptized and join a church. She also presented him with two lovely girls. During the difficult Depression years, it was Caroline who became the human presence of love and support.

The following years were filled with activities and travels. J.C. Penney was in great demand as a speaker and lecturer. He also preached in a number of churches, including the

First Congregational Church of Hollywood and the First Baptist Church of Dallas, Texas.

He continued to serve on the Board of Directors of the Penney Retirement Community (which was named that after his death). Mr. Penney was forced to give up their place in White Plains, New York, because the city condemned it in order to use the land for a high school. He and Caroline bought an apartment in Manhattan which had four bedrooms, kitchen, living room, dining room, library, sitting room and rooms for domestic help. They also owned the Greens Farm in Connecticut where he was able to keep in touch with the farm life he loved.

J.C. Penney lived a disciplined life, reading his devotional book, with his Bible, several news magazines and the hometown paper from Hamilton, Missouri. Frequently he and Caroline went to the opera and he even enjoyed listening to rock and roll music on his stereo.

Each winter the couple went to Palm Beach, Florida, and always stopped at Penney Farms to visit the place he loved so dearly. Today there are still residents there who remember Mr. Penney's visits and how young he seemed as he entered the senior years of his life. His maturing was in Christian faith and action but it still manifested ideas which came out of the conservative background of his days in Missouri.

One person at Penney Farms told of a visit by Mr. Penney when he spotted a maintenance man smoking while cutting grass around the buildings. He asked someone for his name and then contacted the director of maintenance and ordered him to fire the man.

Another story is told about Mr. Penney having a luncheon appointment with a man who was being interviewed for a possible executive position in the company. When this man reached for the salt shaker before tasting his food, Mr. Penney decided he would not hire him because he didn't taste the food first and demonstrate his ability to do the right thing first.

Though negative stories appear concerning famous people and how human they are, there are also inspiring stories of people like J.C. Penney. One of these comes from Les Smith, a resident at Penney Retirement Community since 1978. Mr. Smith worked as a salesman for the J.C. Penney store in Lima, Ohio. He was assigned to the shoe department. One day while he was fitting a 49-cent pair of sneakers to a boy, the manager came up with another person behind him.

"Mr. Smith," the manager said, with Les wondering what he had done wrong in that department, "I want you to meet Mr. J.C. Penney." The distinguished visitor shook his hand warmly while the manager informed him that there was going to be a meeting with Mr. Penney after the nine o'clock closing.

As all the employees gathered, Les noticed that Mr. Penney sat at a desk, in the front, with Tom Zupor, the manager of the store. Then the manager asked, "Is there anyone here who can lead us in some hymn singing?"

One employee raised his hand and said he was a choir leader at a local church. Then, for a half hour, the employees joined in singing old familiar hymns from memory. This was followed by a brief talk by J.C. Penney which recounted some of the high points of his spiritual journey.

Mr. Smith said, "There wasn't one word said that could be construed to either be better salespeople or to accept Christ and His Church. It was the kind of experience one would never forget."

Bascom Franklin, who worked with Penney for so many years, later told how he, like so many business executives, appeared, during his working time, to be cold while manifesting super abilities but in fact he was warm toward people. He had a tremendous capacity for remembering names and made a point to visit whomever happened to be sick.

Employees of the J.C. Penney Corporation in New York City gathered in 1971 to celebrate J.C. Penney's ninety-fifth birthday. It was a joyful occasion, with some relatives and friends there. Caroline, who was at his side for forty-five years, joined with him in hoping he could live to be one hundred and celebrate their golden wedding anniversary with her.

At the birthday party the master of ceremonies said, "Today, at the age of ninety-five, James Cash Penney stands alone as the last of the early 'merchant princes.' His eyesight may be somewhat impaired but he has said, 'My vision is greater than ever,' and his body may be weakened but he walks stronger than ever...HE THINKS YOUNG, HE ACTS YOUNG, EVEN AT NINETY-FIVE HE IS YOUNG!"

In the J.C. Penney company paper, *The Penney News*, Mr. Penney wrote an article that week where he said, "I am presently in my 96th year. Through the grace of God, I have been permitted to experience one of the most exciting, phenomenal and revolutionary periods in the history of the world...all through those times of building the company I devoted nearly all my energy to my company business...when I had my break-down I found it was caused by my paralysis of the spirit. Upon coming out of this, I suddenly learned to pray and in so doing I submitted myself to the will of God. My spiritual life had been stored away in a separate compartment and God had little opportunity to shape my daily thinking."

James Cash Penney died on February 14, 1971, in the Columbia Presbyterian Hospital in New York City. A memorial service was held in the St. James Episcopal Church in New York and he was buried in the Woodlawn Cemetery.

Dr. Norman Vincent Peale, a friend and admirer of Mr. Penney, offered the prayer in which he said, "We lift our gratitude to Thee, O God, because James Cash Penney was never victimized by success nor fame to grow arrogant or selfish.

"Rather did he ever become humble with a disarming wonderment about him that those great things could have happened to him, thy servant James, O Lord, for all his superlative gifts of mind and heart, he remained to the last a humble unaffected child of God, all of which made us love him the more, and his benefactions and good work shall ever bless his name!"

A memorial service was also held at the Penney Memorial Church at Penney Farms which he had built in the midst of the retirement community which is committed to carrying on the spirit and energy of his dedicated life.

At that service the residents involved were remembering what his sacrifices on their behalf had meant to all who had retired and found new ways to keep young as he had. They were thinking about the tribute paid to him concerning, "thinking young, acting young, and being young."

In 1998, in special recognition of those at Penney Retirement Community, who had lived to be ninety or older, a large number of residents gathered to pay them honor. There were fifty-two people ranging in ages from ninety to ninety-six who attended. Many of these were still active in the clubs, the church, the tennis games, the swimming pool and a variety of other social activities on campus and off campus. They were living testimonies to J.C. Penney who maintained his alertness and vitality until the fall which put him into the hospital for the last days.

On September 16, 1975, the members of the Penney Retirement Community held a service in their church remembering that it was the 100th anniversary of J.C. Penney's birth.

Amongst the many aspects of the service was the reading of a portion from the Twenty-sixth Psalm. "I have trusted in the Lord without wavering, prove me, O Lord, and try me; test my heart and my mind. For your steadfast love is before my eyes, and I will walk in faithfulness to You."

Dr. Willis M. Lewis, a resident of that community and a retired army chaplain said, "Mr. Penney's witness was what it says in that verse—it was also his faith."

Epilogue

Grampa and Grandma were excited because their daughter, Faith, was arriving with her husband, Dexter, and their ten-year-old daughter, Susan. It was the first time they would see the Penney Retirement Community in Penney Farms, Florida. The most rewarding part of their trip from Connecticut was to bring a load of furniture for Grampa and Grandma's new home on the retirement community's campus. Grampa had just retired after a long stay in the New England area.

The retired couple had arrived in April 1997, two days earlier, and were making certain that the cottage on Ott Avenue was ready. The maintenance department had painted the entire interior, new carpeting had been laid, and a new room was added to the sixty-two-year-old cottage, to provide more adequate space and personal comforts. The new residents stayed at the Guest House on campus and ate in the Quadrangle Dining Room where they met some residents for the first time.

Other residents had contacted the new couple upon hearing of their arrival. They offered to help with the settling of furniture and whatever other needs might arise. Grampa assured them that he and the son-in-law could pretty well unload the truck, except the piano which would require some extra strong hands and backs. Several of the men assured him that, though they were retired, they had engaged in every kind of physical activity on campus and were most willing to lend their strength to fulfill Grampa's need for his piano. They gave their phone numbers and promised to be on the alert for the arrival of the rented moving vehicle.

In the middle of the sunny April day, the yellow rented moving truck with three wide-eyed occupants drew up in front of the administration office. They were directed to the Guest House where Grandma and Grampa were patiently waiting to welcome them to Penney Farms.

After warm hugs, kisses and exclamations of enthusiasm by the trio, with expressed appreciation for the beautiful campus which they entered on Daniel Poling Boulevard, they headed down Caroline Avenue to the newly acquired cottage of Grandma and Grampa. Susan spoke of how beautiful the golf course was and expressed interest in learning to play golf. Her parents liked the entrance and told how inspiring it was to see the palm trees lining the streets with huge, spreading live oaks shading the houses. Magnolia trees were planted everywhere they looked. The granddaughter and her parents told the grandparents that they had expected a typical high-rise, institutional type of retirement center. Little did they expect what appeared to be a college campus with connecting walks, and buildings of all types and sizes designed in French-Norman style. What really impressed them were people walking, riding bicycles and tricycles, as well as golf carts. Everywhere they looked they saw movement and as Dexter said, "And it's not 'rocking-chair' movement."

Drawing up in front of the residence where Grandma and Grampa were going to spend their next years, they saw a unique, red-tile roofed house, with stucco exterior and a glassed-in porch facing the street. Other similar cottages were joined together in clusters of four, giving a picture of a village with community ties. Newly trimmed bushes and colorful flower gardens outlining the buildings gave one the impression that beauty was a big part of communal caring. Though this retirement community was created in 1926-1927 by J.C. Penney, it was different from any of those in existence because it was made to look like a classic European village.

Grampa and Grandma hurried over to their cottage on their bikes and drew up behind the rented moving truck with excited anticipation. Other neighbors appeared, as if by magic, to welcome the new residents and to offer assistance in unloading the truck.

Before late evening set in, everything had been put in its place along with the piano and the usual overload of boxes. Faith, Dexter and Susan were impressed by the interior of the house: the high cathedral ceiling in the living room; the fireplace, which Grampa explained once heated the house; the cozy little kitchen with cabinets, stove, refrigerator and sink; and the alcove off the living room which served as the bedroom for the previous occupants, but now had a Murphy bed for guests. A small dining room connecting the kitchen and living room was just the place for a dropped-leaf table and matching chairs. The new bedroom off the living room was large and roomy. In addition to the bed and bureaus it had room enough for a desk and file drawers.

As daughter Faith began to help Grandma unpack boxes, she remarked that she was pleased with how adequate the cottage seemed to be for her parents. Grampa reminded her that as each new couple moved in they made their desired improvements which were then passed on to the next residents to succeed them.

The five of them had their first meal on the screened porch, enjoying the squirrels who seemed to be checking on the new residents. Though some boxes were still awaiting attention the appearance of normalcy surfaced and it was already beginning to feel like home.

The beige-carpeted living room had a new sofa and two reclining chairs, the ever-present television set, an antique dish closet, lamps, end tables, bookcases, and rocking chair which had belonged to Grandma's mother.

Faith and Dexter slept on the pull-out Murphy bed in the alcove, while Grampa and Grandma slept in the new bedroom enjoying the brand-new bed and bureaus which had been purchased in Orange Park, twenty miles away, and delivered on the Monday before.

As they set up a cot borrowed from a neighbor for Susan to sleep on, Grampa said, "You may be surprised to know that some of the couples who moved into these cottages in 1927 had children just like you, Susan."

"I thought this was built just for old people."

"It was, but when it was first started, way back then, some ministers who had health problems or were without work in a church were permitted to come here temporarily. So, they had to put up cots for the children. One family had four boys."

Susan gasped, "And how did they fit them into a cottage like this?"

"In that day people lived in smaller homes and were accustomed to having less space."

Everyone slept well that night even though the temperature had gone up to eighty degrees outside. The central air and fans provided them with air circulation and the quietness outside was only touched by the solo of a chuck-will's-widow which is a member of the whippoorwill family.

Susan exclaimed at breakfast the next morning that she laid awake a long time enjoying the bird's solo and thinking about how lucky Grampa and Grandma were to live in such a place.

After breakfast, which included juicy, fresh grapefruits brought in by a neighbor, Grandma and Grampa took the three members of the family on a tour of the campus.

They wound their way down the walks which connected the houses to each other as though it was a college campus.

The first stop was at the Penney Memorial Church where they read the plaque dedicating it in the name of Mr. Penney's parents. While going through the sanctuary to the lecture room and library, beautiful organ music permeated the rooms.

"That's one of several organists we have here on campus," explained Grandma. "There are so many organists that they allot practice time to each one each day."

"Must mean you have music in here all during the week," said Faith.

"Yes, and it also means that each month we have a different organist. It makes for a wonderful variety of styles."

As they went out the front door, Dexter noticed a list of preachers posted for each Sunday. Grampa explained, "Just a few years after this was built in 1927, the church decided they didn't need a pastor with so many preachers living here, so they began to use a different one each Sunday."

"How many ministers do you have here now?"

Grampa responded, "There are seventy-five, but remember we now have four hundred and fifty residents so they don't control the community—just the pulpit."

The tour continued with a visit to Barrows Hall which had only been built two years before. The Sunshine Band was rehearsing, getting ready to play at the meeting of the Residents Association. They saw the Arts and Crafts building where furniture-building, stained-glass making, weaving on looms, sewing and rug hooking took place. From there they went to the main office and met Dr. Noel White, administrator of the community. He had a picture of Mr. J.C. Penney on the wall of his office.

Susan looked at it intensely and said, "Grampa told us about him last night and how he left the farm in Missouri and went west to start his first stores."

"The wonderful thing about Mr. Penney is that he invested millions of dollars in this place to care for people like your grandmother and grandfather. And he did it as a wonderful Christian concerned for people who needed a place for retirement which offered activities in art, music, handwork, exercise, swimming, golf and deepening of their spiritual lives. In fact Mr. Penney would never have dreamed of all that has happened with these buildings. We have three assisted-living places and a new nursing home called the Pavilion for health care. All these facilities allow freedom for folks to live normal lives."

The rest of the tour included visiting the places that Dr. White had mentioned.

At noon they had a tasty meal in the dining room, located in the newly renovated Christian Herald Quadrangle. They noticed the friendliness and happiness of the people who filled the beautifully decorated room.

That afternoon Susan and her parents went to the swimming pool with Grandma and Grampa. As they sat in the spa enjoying the hot water relaxing their tired muscles, Grandma asked Susan, "Honey, what do you think of this place?"

"Mr. Penney must have been a wonderful man to do all the things he did for others," she responded.

"And one feels his presence here as it's lived out through these happy people," said her dad.

"I wish I'd known him," Susan said. "He sounds totally awesome!"

THE AUTHOR'S RECOMMENDED BIBLIOGRAPHY

The Man with the Thousand Partners: An Autobiography of J.C. Penney as told to Robert Bruere. New York: Harper and Brothers, 1931.

Main Street Merchant: the Story of the J.C. Penney Co. by Norman Beasley. New York: McGraw-Hill Book Company. Whittlesey House, 1948.

My Experience with the Golden Rule by J.C. Penney. Kansas City: Frank Glenn Publishing Company, 1949.

Fifty Years with The Golden Rule by J.C. Penney. New York: Harper and Brothers, 1950.

Lines of a Layman by J.C. Penney. Grand Rapids, Michigan: William B. Eerdmans Publishing Company, 1956.

View from the Ninth Decade: Jottings from a Merchant's Daybook by J.C. Penney. New York: Thomas Nelson and Sons, 1960.

Penney Retirement Community Association: Life More Abundant, 1973. (Available through the Penney Retirement Community Library.)

The Golden Jubilee Celebration of the Penney Retirement Community, published by the Penney Retirement Community, 1975.

Parade of Memories: A History of Clay County, Florida by Arch Frederic Blakey. Jacksonville, Florida: Clay County Board of Commissioners, 1976.

Creating an American Institution: The Merchandising Genius of J.C. Penney by Mary Elizabeth Curry: Garland Publishing, Inc., New York and London, 1993.

Penney Retirement Community — 70th Anniversary: The Past is Prologue by Kenneth Wilson, 1996. (Available through the Penney Retirement Community Library.)